Monica Clarke has dedicated much of her professional and private life to caring for the vulnerable and to raising her voice, as a speaker and a writer, on their behalf.

Born in South Africa, under the Apartheid regime as a member of the indigenous Khoikhoen people, she first qualified as a nurse and a midwife before retraining as a lawyer, specialising in the defence of people prosecuted under South Africa's draconian apartheid laws. Her 50-year career as a political activist and member of the African National Congress resulted in her being sought by the government security services. Monica had to leave her family and go into hiding in order to flee the regime's para-military 'death squads'.

In the 1990s, she was granted political asylum in the UK, where she worked as a commercial lawyer until her psychotherapist husband suffered a major stroke.

Monica gave up her career in order to care for him on a full-time basis. This in turn led her to become a vocal and forceful advocate for the rights of carers and of patients themselves, as well as black and ethnic minorities in the UK.

At the beginning of this Century, following her husband's death, she was recruited as an Associate Director in the NHS Chief Medical Officer's Team dedicated to improvements in the quality of care and in the full and active involvement of patients and carers as 'partners in their own care'.

Following her retirement from the NHS, her ongoing concern for the plight of young people in South Africa led her, in 2013, to found there a Charity 'I Protect Me' (IPM) dedicated to empowering young people with the confidence and the personal skills to defend themselves and their peers from exploitation and abuse.

IPM, of which she remains the Honorary President, has grown into a Pan-African organisation that recruits and supports unemployed trainers to teach prevention of abuse as a life skill in schools, reaching thousands of young people to resist abuse and to change mindsets and cultural inertia to abuse.

Monica continues to be an energetic and persuasive advocate on behalf of the disadvantaged and the oppressed—whether of this or of earlier times.

This book tells the story of one of her Khoikhoen ancestors, whose story has for too long been distorted by a corrupt and partial historical record that abuses her memory, just as her captors abused her in her tragically short life. It is homage to a remarkable woman—Saartjie Baartman.

Monica lives in London, UK, with her husband, Hedley Bennett "The wind beneath my sails," as Monica says.

I dedicate this book to my children, Darroll and Celeste, who endured long hours without my attention whilst I burnt the midnight oil.

To my ancestors, the KhoiKhoi, I give thanks for your wisdom and protection of me and my offspring.

With Respect,

Monica

Monica Clarke

Hottentot Venus – The Story of Saartjie Baartman

Austin Macauley Publishers
LONDON · CAMBRIDGE · NEW YORK · SHARJAH

Copyright © Monica Clarke 2023

The right of Monica Clarke to be identified as author of this work has been asserted by the author in accordance with sections 77 and 78 of the Copyright, Designs and Patents Act 1988.

All rights reserved. No part of this publication may be reproduced, stored in a retrieval system, or transmitted in any form or by any means, electronic, mechanical, photocopying, recording, or otherwise, without the prior permission of the publishers.

Any person who commits any unauthorised act in relation to this publication may be liable to criminal prosecution and civil claims for damages.

All of the events in this memoir are true to the best of the author's memory. The views expressed in this memoir are solely those of the author.

A CIP catalogue record for this title is available from the British Library.

ISBN 9781035818037 (Paperback)
ISBN 9781035818044 (ePub e-book)

www.austinmacauley.com

First Published 2023
Austin Macauley Publishers Ltd®
1 Canada Square
Canary Wharf
London
E14 5AA

Inspite of all of the vicissitudes I have encountered, I am indeed a woman blessed with family, friends and colleagues, who have been supportive of me throughout my life.

I particularly wish to thank Yvette Abrahams and Diana Ferrus, my two Khoikhoen sisters, who recorded Saartjie's story with the feeling and respect which our historical ancestor, Saartjie, deserves. Your poems and stories have helped me to take courage, to try to join you in rewriting our history, and to contradict the opinions of other writers over two centuries, onlookers before you, who have written Saartjie's story, often maligning her, without acknowledging the great beauty of our common cultural heritage.

My colleague Professor Paul Stanton, my Encourager, I thank you for your wisdom and guidance and to Dr Pip Hardy and Tony Sumner, of Pilgrim Projects, a special thanks for believing in me, and for helping me by making a digital story of this great ancestor of mine, when the idea for the book was yet just a plan developing in my head.

Read More at *www.MonicaClarke.website*

Table of Contents

Introduction	13
Prologue	16
Portsmouth, England	19
Shall I or Shall I Not?	28
The Exhibition	32
Nature Mother	41
The English People	43
Zachary Macaulay	46
Lies, Lies, Lies	50
Questions, Questions, Questions	55
Final Departure	62
Paris	68
On Becoming a Woman	75
!Habab	78
Rain	86

Tata Is Dead	**95**
Pieter Cezars	**101**
Cape Town	**106**
Paddy	**110**
Paddy Leaves	**116**
Destiny	**121**
Birth	**126**
The Husband	**130**
Themba	**133**
Grief	**137**
Epilogue	**148**
Tribute to a Grandmother	**149**
Who were the KhoiKhoi?	**162**
Further Reading	**169**
Endnotes	**171**

Everything in the world, natural and supernatural, possesses vital force. And its importance or unimportance in life depends on how much vital force it has.
You are safe only for so long as you are in your place of birth and when you leave it, you are in danger.
Worldview of the Khoi[1]
The only history of a country is to be found in its newspapers
Lord Macaulay, 1811[2]
©Copyright Monica Clarke

Introduction

In the year 1810, Saartjie Baartman was stowed away on a ship by a British army surgeon and his South African business partner and taken to Britain, and then to France, to be put on display in exhibition halls. She thought she was going overseas to be a nursery maid. She ended in bonded labour.

Does this still sound familiar today?

Saartjie was a woman of the indigenous people of South Africa. Her story is the story of all colonised aboriginal peoples the world over: a story of endless and still unending systematic physical, psychological and emotional abuse.[3] Saartjie's story is particularly relevant today, when human trafficking and bonded labour are on a frightening increase,[4] this more than 200 years after her death.

This book is written in language which is easy to read.

I am a direct descendent of Saartjie. I decided to write this book speaking through the mouth and eyes of Saartjie herself, as she will have experienced her life.

I have learned so much from her. She has a lot to teach, not only to the young adult professional of tomorrow whose work will involve vigilance of human rights abuses, but also to scholars of humanities and social sciences and the ordinary reader who has a commitment to, understand and then to guard against, abuse and violence.

We are born into our social circumstances and most of our choices in life are dictated by those circumstances.

Saartjie's choices were severely limited from the first by immense historical, political and social pressures, and by changes over her short life. Nonetheless, she took responsibility for her own actions. In this, as in much else, she is a lesson to all of us.

This is not the first book about her life. So why, then, another book about Saartjie Baartman? Because 'the more we study how her life unfolded, and what kinds of choices she was able to make, the more we begin to understand about our own lives and times. She illuminates our on challenges and dilemmas. In understanding her, we gain power over our own lives.'[5] Saartjie's story is about the buying and selling of human beings, about abuse by the powerful of the vulnerable.

I wrote this book because I believe that we all and have a duty to speak up against violence, abuse and prejudice, against demeaning language, jokes, the use of stereotypes, against discrimination and oppression of any type or form.

Saartjie stood no chance in 1810. I have been more fortunate. I can borrow her voice and use her story to speak up for those who were abused then, and for all of those who are suffering and bleeding more than two hundred years later.

Saartjie's life changed completely when she met Alexander Dunlop, a Scottish doctor, who was working as a ship's surgeon for the British Army. This was her chief misfortune.

There are few historical records of the lives of individual Khoikhoen,[6] and no birth records of them have been kept. The history of Saartjie in South Africa before she went to Europe is, therefore, not recorded. The experiences she tells of her life in South Africa in this narrative are scenes I have constructed from historical records relating to the life of the Khoikhoen. I have based these on historical fact, as recorded by observers at the time. The name Thandi has been given by me to Saartjie as her birthname. This is an assumed name, in the same way that the name Saartjie Baartman and other names are adopted names given to her by the Dutch at the Cape, and the British after she was taken to England.

All the people in this book whom Saartjie met in Europe actually made contact with her during her time there. Their names and characters are real. The essence of conversations is true. The actual words which passed between people have sometimes been reconstructed, but most conversations which took place in England and France have been transcribed from written records, especially from transcripts of court proceedings and newspapers of the time.[7] They tell a horrifying story—all the more disturbing because women, men and children in the 21st Century still undergo similar cruel and inhumane ordeals.

Prologue

He gives me brandy. This makes my head swim, and I see things.

I need something to help me with the fever, but the new man—the animal keeper—will not give me anything but brandy.

This makes the dream creep into my day thoughts, like a snake looking for the warmth of the sun. And the pain is deep, coming from the angry souls of my ancestors to punish me.

The dream always happens in the garden which I can see from my window before I go to sleep. There are saws. There are knives. There are scissors. Cutting and clipping, blood flowing over my private parts. Always my private parts, sometimes my brain, all put into jars standing on the side[8].

But the worst part is the boiling of bones. My bones, taken out of my body, dropped into a pot.

"Bones must be boiled in caustic potash for several hours to remove the flesh, after which they must be put in a bag," I hear the Doctor of Science tell his prattling helpers. It is my bones which he is talking about. He throws them into a seething mixture, a witch's cauldron.

The sound of my screams pierces my eardrums and I toss in my sleep, a heavy hand holding me down. I sweat, and then

I come to rest. All my body parts come to rest, laid out on shelves inside that large science room of the dead in the garden in Paris.

My body parts lie there in my dream, next to three Egyptian mummies, an Italian, a dwarf. Thousands of hands, feet, hips, legs. And bones. Back bones, shoulder bones, big body bones, small body bones. And 2,000 skulls. Luckily, in my dream, my head is not sawn off. But the Doctor of Science does cut the skin in a circle around my scalp and opens my skull to get my brain out.

"Heads of savages, covered in their own desiccated and tattooed skin, important for scientific study," he mumbles, pulling the skin off my head—off my whole body—and the pain burns so great that I scream in my dream.

My body burns with fever every day. But this scorching pain in my dream is worse, much worse.

I must be patient, as my Tata,[9] taught me. I can do it.

Sometimes I have to stand in front of the gawking crowds all day, from morning till night. It is very hard. But I will keep trying, although I know now that I will never get the money they promised me, because Hendrick[10] has taken it all back to Cape Town with him. I had hoped to buy new arrowheads for my young brother, Bhundi, with the money.

Perhaps I will still get some money. This is why I keep standing, keep hoping. So long as they don't touch me.

What else can I do?

This morning, before the day started, I was sitting on the floor with my eyes closed, hoping the brandy would take away the pain, for the boils throb with fever. But the brandy did not help today.

Instead, sitting there on the floor, evil spirits appeared in my throbbing head. They filled my room and I lay down again, as they started to mock me.

They whispered that I drank too much. They teased me. They closed my eyes and told me that white medicine men, many of them, will come to see me. White men in white coats, with little black books.

"They will look at you through eyeglasses. They will poke you, pull on you, measure you in this strange land," the spirits squealed at me in my half-awake state "and then they will kill you!"

Then I woke up, sweating. The first thing I did was to reach for the *eau de vie*—water of life, as the French call the brandy.

Then I took the necklace which Solkar[11] had given me, brought it to my lips, and prayed to my ancestors for forgiveness.

Portsmouth, England

I came from my hot country to that cold country on a ship.[12] We used to see the same ship in Cape Town. It carried soldiers.

But I did not leave on the ship from Cape Town. I was taken to Saldanha Bay. Near there, the water boils in a long line as the two big seas meet. I was afraid that the ship might fall over when it goes over the boiling water. Luckily this did not happen.

There were only men on the ship. I was the only one who had to sleep underneath, with the bags of grain. No light, no sun, for a very long time. They left my food and water on the floor and did not speak with me. To keep warm, I slept under the bag with the skin of a camelopard,[13] which Hendrick told me to look after.

I was scared to go to stay in a new country. But I was also excited. There are so many new things to see and learn. But I know now there is also lots of loneliness.

I feel like I am always sitting with people who see me, but don't see me. They talk about friends, family, about how it was when they were young, in fast language which is hard to understand. They talk about places with strange names. And I sit there, hearing them while I watch and listen to the birds who, like me, have travelled from far, across the seas. The birds say that they, like me, are just passing through.

I do not like the smell of this country called England. It does not smell good. It stinks of rotten fish and unwashed people. The harbour where we arrived with the ship was filled with naked bodies of slaves who were unloading big bags of broken dreams onto an unsympathetic, hard earth.

I was carrying my trunk. The skirt I was wearing, which Hendrick's wife, Anna Catharina, had given me, was stiff because I had slept in it for so many nights.

Even the sun was unwilling, pale and unfriendly.

Then I saw Hendrick. He saw me too, but he just turned around and walked away from me when he saw me.

"Kom!"—come! he called into the widening gap between us, which quickly filled up with people. I could not keep up with him. I stumbled, because I could not see where I put my feet under the big brown skirt with its unnecessary petticoats dragging through grey dust. The wooden ramp splintered spitefully under my bare foot, and I cried out in pain. But there was no time to stop. I stumbled forward.

When we came out into the street, an old slave came up to me and roughly took my trunk. He did not speak to me.

Already I was missing my family.

But the people were so different that I soon forgot how tired I was. The way they dressed was silly, the men with their wigs and the women with high collars and funny hair. Their high, round, thick hair looked like birds' nests, tied with ribbons to keep the sea winds out. I thought that there might be little birds in there, for the sea gulls swooped around and I thought they might peck on the bits of glass decorating the women's hair.

Their language, too, was different. I enjoyed their highs and lows, mumbles and throat-sounds, which were different from the way the English language was spoken at home.

The old slave man left me standing in front of a tavern. I admired the different vehicles with fancy trimmings, and rich people sitting on high seats above wheels twice my size.

I started to feel important. I had crossed the seas after all, and I was part of a modern world at last. I watched the drivers who were waiting. There were armed guards who stood slightly away from everyone else. The noise and the movement of the crowd made the horses nervous.

The slave man came back to me and took me to a coach. It was brightly painted and pulled four horses, which were keen to be on their way. The coach was splattered with mud.

There was space for only six people inside. It was full of fat, loud women sitting on cushioned seats next to grumbling husbands with wet coughs, who ignored them.

The old slave climbed up past them, then clambered over the people on the roof, and reached down for me from behind the coach. The poorest of the poor were sitting on the roof. I, poorer than the poor, had to sit at the back, in a huge basket pulled on wheels.

The journey was uncomfortable and dangerous. People around me were talking constantly. Some of them drank from bottles. They did not speak to me, but they did not treat me unkindly either. I was happy to sit amongst them, in the noise, for I was part of their big world. I heard them speak nervously of highwaymen as we travelled through wooded areas.

There were so many people on the roof that the coach seemed to want to turn over each time it went around a corner. It often went off the road. In most places, the road was no more than a dirt track. It might have been better to walk beside it, for it was going so slowly.

On the way to London, we had to get off the coach twice to push it up a hill. The horses were not as strong as our oxen back home, which can pull wagons through mountains without stopping. The sun and the moon exchanged places two times, and we were still on the road.

Not that we could see the sun, which lingered out of sight, like a frightened fox waiting for the hounds to go by before it showed its face. I slept, woke up, slept again.

At last, we arrived in the big city of London. We had to push through the crowds, and the shouting, jostling and madness of street London made my insides quiver. We were bumped into and pushed from all sides. The people hustled and shouted, selling, bartering, and dealing with lecherous looks, covering their hunger with joviality.

The loudness and vulgarity attacked my ears.

A black boy was waiting for us when we got off the coach. He had a bright, smiley face.

"Good morning," he said brightly. I smiled faintly at him. Those were the first kind words anyone had spoken to me since I arrived.

We walked to a very smart place, past a park. I could hear the chimes of a big clock as we went through the back of a big house. I did not take to the house. It was made of ugly bricks. It looked familiar to me, like some of the houses in the centre of Cape Town, on the Heerengracht, the main street. But even if they looked the same, these houses did not have the bright, sunlit faces of the big houses in Cape Town, like the one where I used to work in before I went to live with Hendrick.

The boy led me through a side entrance, past the kitchen and stables where the horses were kept. We climbed the dark stairs onto a narrow landing. There were five doors there. The slave left my trunk outside one of these rooms and opened the door.

"Good day," he said again, politely, and I nodded and smiled into his bright black eyes as he walked away.

I went into the room, where there was a bed. I did not like to sleep on a bed, so I took my *kaross*[14] out of my trunk and slept under it on the floor. I slept through the night, I was so tired.

The next morning I was called to help to serve breakfast in the big house. I made out like I did not know what anyone was saying. What they did not know was that I could understand some English. I could even speak some English, but I did not want to let them know.

"Don't say you can speak their language before you know them," my sister Bithathe had warned me. "That way you can find out much about them before they find out about you."

The boy had told me that a famous man would come to visit, a Mr Bullock[15]. When I went into the big room that morning, they were all there together. Hendrick was there. And the doctor. I knew the doctor from Cape Town. His name was Doctor Dunlop. Alexander Dunlop. He was Hendrick's friend and he used to work in the hospital belonging to the British army. I never trusted him. I never liked him.

The slave told me to stand by the big cupboard in the corner and wait until they asked me to take things to them at the table.

I heard what they said. I did not understand everything, but I heard.

"I have brought the camelopard skin which you said you would like to put on display," the doctor Dunlop said to the visitor. "I shall show it to you later in the morning, when we've had a chance to air it!" he said with a short laugh.

He and Hendrick glanced at me. I dropped my eyes onto the silver strips of sun dancing about on the old carpet in time to the swing of the curtains through the open windows.

"I also have another specimen for you besides the giraffe skin." Again they looked in my direction and I felt uncomfortable.

"Oh? What specimen is that?" asked Mr Bullock.

"Well…" The doctor's voice trailed off, as he glanced at me again.

"Saartjie, will you please go and see to the tea!" Hendrick barked at me, and I left the room.

But I was very curious and wanted to know what they were talking about, so I stood quietly on the other side of the open door.

"It is a great curiosity, a most interesting specimen," Dunlop said.

"Yes?" Bullock sounded interested.

"It is a Hottentot[16] woman from the Cape of Good Hope."

Dunlop was speaking very fast, and it took me a while to understand what he was saying. Even then I did not know that he was talking about me.

"A woman!" I heard the surprise and distress in Mr Bullock's voice.

"Anyone might make a fortune in two years by exhibiting her." Dunlop spoke very fast. "And she would be of immense financial advantage to you. Should you make me a handsome offer, I shall let you have the skin and the woman at a bargain.

The woman is of extraordinary shape and make and she is an object of great curiosity, and…"

I heard someone shuffling and I knew that Mr Bullock had stood up, so I hurried away from the door, as he said, loudly, with anger in his voice, "I am interested in exhibiting the woman—any person…"

They were talking about me!

The shock was very great. I did not know what to think. I went to the kitchen and stood dead still, until I heard Mr Bullock leave the house. Then I went back to my room.

And I remembered the day it was decided in the *kraal*[17] that I come here, as clearly as if it had happened yesterday. That day the *Kaptein*[18] called all the elders together with my family. They all came to meet Hendrick, to hear what Hendrick had asked, so they could all decide if I should go across the seas to and work.

Everyone was there, and they all decided that it was good for the people of other lands to get to know our people, the First Race, Men of Men.

It was good for us to step into the shoes of our ancestors, the *Kaptein* said, like Herry, our famous ancestor, who travelled on ships far away, and could speak many languages.

The whole family thought it was a good thing. Paddy was there as well and he promised when I come to this country, he would come and look for me. (I'll tell you about Paddy later, because it is too painful for me to even say his name just now).

But nobody said I was to be sold to anybody. I then remembered what Pieter Cezars, Hendrick's brother, had said that day.

Pieter had sounded worried. "Have you gone to get the permission of Lord Caledon?" he had asked Hendrick as the

Kaptein walked away. I knew why Pieter had asked this. It is because the law said that we, the Khoikhoen (*Hotnots* as they call us), were the children of the Governor of the Cape and only he could give permission for us to travel away from our place of work.

"Not yet," I heard Hendrick say that day. "But I will do that before we go."

"It's very important. There will be big trouble if you try to take Saartjie away without the permission of the Governor," Pieter said again.

"Don't worry. Everything is in order. I have seen to everything," Hendrick said. And we were all happy that he had seen to everything.

I now think that he was telling lies.

"You will be rich," Bithathe had laughed, and Pieter Cezars laughed with us. He said that I would probably come back and buy his small holding.

All arrangements for my journey were made by Hendrick.

But things changed as soon as I stepped onto the ship in Saldanha Bay. Hendrick changed. He was so good to me in Cape Town before we left. He was so nice to me, and I had forgotten how scared I had at first been of him.

I have often wondered why he did not let me get on the ship at Cape Town harbour, for then all my family would have come to say goodbye to me.

Soon Obi,[19] the boy who had first greeted me, came to my room to fetch me. He gestured that I should put on my cloak and go for a walk with him. He smiled a lot and had to walk slowly to keep up with me, because my feet were still sore from walking bare foot. We walked through the park. He stayed close to me, walking almost protectively near me. This made me feel good.

We watched a black boy, a rabbit seller[20], who was standing with his back to us in front of an open door. He knelt down to reach for a dead rabbit from a basket at the feet of a white woman, who was facing the street, her back to the open door. A man was standing behind the woman in the doorway, grinning.

"O la, how it smells," the woman protested, waving her hand in front of her nose as the rabbit seller held it up by its feet. "Sure it's not fresh," she said, turning up her nose.

"Dat no fair, missie," the rabbit seller replied. He looked over his shoulder and saw us and grinned. I could not help but grin back.

The woman waved her hand in front of her face again, then pinched her nose in a comical way.

"How it does smell!" she said again.

"Dat no fair, missie," the rabbit seller repeated. He was holding the rabbit by one hind leg, splayed open. He pushed it further towards the woman's face.

"If black man take you by leg so, you smell too!" he said, turning directly to me with a broad smile.

I grinned. I had understood every word. I belonged.

"What a cheek!" I heard the woman say as she turned angrily and pushed past the man into the house.

Obi was doubled up with laughter and I could not help but join him.

Obi reminded me of my young brother and of my family, and life suddenly seemed brighter.

Shall I or Shall I Not?

Slavery is a life of control: control of movement, of living, of thinking. That Saartjie was coerced into the exhibition I have little doubt. It is recorded that she thought she was going to Europe to be a nursery maid. In this chapter, I have constructed the circumstances which led to her unfortunate decision.

> Mungo, a black slave, sang in 1800:
> *Dear Heart! What a terrible Life am I led?*
> *A Dog has a better that's tethered and fed;*
> *Night and Day tis the same. My Pain is dere Game*
> *Me wish to the Lord me was dead.*
>
> *What'er's to be done, Poor Black must run*
> *Mungo here, Mungo, Mungo everywhere.*
> *Above or below, Sirrah, come, Sirrah, go;*
> *Do so, and do so. Oh! Oh!*
> *Me wish to the Lord me was dead.*[21]

In London that very first day, when I got back to the house, Hendrick asked me to show myself. I had not thought that Hendrick would ask me this. My family had not agreed that I come to show my body.

Hendrick sent the boy to call me. I went back into the big room with the big chairs. The doctor was there as well.

"Things have changed," Hendrick said into his beard, not looking at me, but speaking in Dutch so that only I could understand him.

I did not say anything.

"There is no work here for you. There are no children to look after," he said, still not looking at me. "We want you to show your body to the people." He looked over to the doctor, who was staring out of the big round window onto the street. The doctor could still not understand the Dutch language which we spoke, even though he had lived in Cape Town for many years himself!

I frowned, said nothing. I was too shocked. The reason why I came was to be a nursery maid! My breasts were still letting out milk, even though I had stopped feeding the baby, Hendrick and Catharina's baby.

"But I thought I was going to be a wet nurse…," my voice trailed off when I saw the stubborn look on his face.

He glared at me, and I went quiet. I knew Hendrick for many years. I know how brutal he can be. I am afraid of his temper.

"And you will show yourself!" he shouted.

"No, no, no, I will not do that!" I could not stop myself from screaming.

The doctor then called Hendrick over, and they spoke with each other in English, which they thought I could not understand.

"Tell her that she will get much more money if she shows herself. Tell her nursery maids do not earn much money," the doctor said.

"You will get more money if you show yourself," Hendrick repeated to me like the puppet that he was.

"Tell her that I promise to keep half of all the money for her, that I will send her back after two years, and that I will pay for her passage back."

"We will give you half the money," Hendrick repeated in Dutch, "and we will pay for you to go back to Cape Town after two years."

"Tell her that all we are asking is that she plays on her *ramkie*, dances and shows what a great people the Khoi are!"

This time I looked directly at the doctor, but I did not answer. Maybe it was true that if I showed these people in this foreign land what a proud people my people are, sang our music to them, that they would think a lot of me, and of my people.

Also, it is polite to entertain visitors. We always do this. We sing and dance whenever someone comes to visit. This is nothing unusual. And if it means that I would get more money doing this, I kept telling myself, that is not such a bad idea after all. I will be helping these people to hear about my people, the Khoi, Men of Men, what a proud nation we are. And it would be good for them to hear our music, and learn about our customs, I thought.

I did not answer directly but I did not refuse. I swear by the great one Heitsi-Eibib, who stands like a dawn tree listening to everything, I swear that I never agreed to the horrible things I was told to do after that.

It was only later that Hendrick would make me take my *kaross* off and to put on the light, silk dress which, because it was the same colour as my skin, people could see through.

And I never expected to stand inside a metal cage on a wooden stage. But Hendrick said if I did not obey him, he would leave me and I would not have any food to eat.

So I had to do it.

I kept telling myself that it was not such a bad idea after all. I was helping these people to hear about my people, the Khoi, and it would be good for them to hear our music, and learn about our customs, I thought.

The Exhibition

'The result of white men's obsession with Sarah Bartmann's body is that there are large parts of her history I simply cannot write' (Yvette Abrahams).[22]

I miss my family, my two brothers and three sisters. Most of all I miss Bithathe, my eldest sister. All I long for is to go home again to my family.

And I miss Anna Catharina too. I had nursed her babies for her for many years, and I loved her babies. She used to be a slave, but then she was made free. She and Hendrick Cezars got married when he became a free man. He left Anna Catharina behind when he came to England and I wish she had come along with him.

Anna Catharina was always good to me. I wish I could see her again, so that I can show her that I still have the big skirt which she lent to me to wear on the boat.

But Hendrick has changed so much, I doubt if Anna Catharina would still want to be married to him. Now that he is a freeman, he thinks he is a boss, but it cannot change the fact that he is still like all of us. In fact, he forgets that we, the KhoiKhoi, have never even been slaves! Now he thinks he is better than me, threatening me all the time. He is very unkind, never a kind word to me.

I did start showing myself in that place called London, that very next week. I was too scared to refuse. At first it was not too difficult, because I could play on my *ramkie*[23] and sing while I was doing this. But when he took my *ramkie* away and made me turn this way and that way for hours on end, I became very fed up and angry. And I showed him how angry I was, but it made no difference.

How I felt did not matter to him, so long as he got the money from those people who were happy to come and stare at me. All of them were happy, and it did not matter to them how I felt.

One day, many moons later, I was still standing there, stared at for hours on end in that big exhibition hall, which was full of people, who came there when they left the museum, the William Bullock Museum.

I stood for six hours a day and people came to stare at me, passing remarks all the time, which they thought I could not understand. Sometimes Hendrick would allow me to play my little *ramkie*. I loved feeling the dried pumpkin skin against my hands, which were now going soft because I was not doing proper woman's work. I loved to play on the three gut strings, holding it under my chin, smelling it, and singing. Those were the best times.

At other times, he took the *ramkie* away from me. He made me smoke a pipe and blow smoke over the crowd. He painted my face in a funny way. This I was not used to. We never painted our faces back home. I felt ridiculous. And Obi, the boy, laughed at me when he came one day with Hendrick.

But the worst times were later in the day, when the men came to stare at me. Then I had to come out of the cage and walk about in front of the rows of men—and turn when he ordered me to.

One afternoon a famous actor came to stand by the cage[24] I was being shown in. His name was John Kemble.[25] Obi told me his name the next day, because it was in the newspapers.

I was very cold[26] and had my arms around me, although Hendrick had told me many times not to do this. When Hendrick saw me put my arms around me, he shouted at me in Dutch, and the famous man heard him, so I dropped my arms.

"What a disgusting sight," I heard John Kemble say. He must have thought I could not understand him, for he mumbled to a woman standing next to him, "I feel so sorry, so deeply sorry for her."

I was very tired. By this time I had been standing for more than five hours, and I needed to sleep. With great effort, I pulled my back straight and wriggled my body as I tried to shift more comfortably into the knee-length dress which pulled tightly around me, showing every bump, every fold of me.

I sighed. Every time I took a deep breath, my chest strained against the tight bodice and my breasts flattened against the see-through fabric. My two nipples spread out flat, gaping at the crowd, like two blobs of black gum pressed out under the glass of a microscope. I felt shy and embarrassed.

"Forward!" I heard Hendrick shout from behind the curtain, where nobody could see him. He said this in a loud voice, so everyone could hear him.

"Like a wild beast being ordered around," I heard John Kemble mutter again, but I could not see his face, for I had turned away from him, "more like a bear on a chain than a human being," he said, for I was totally under Hendrick's command and afraid of what he would do if I did not obey.

I knew that John Kemble was looking at me from behind, and I felt hot with shame.

"*Draai!*" Turn! Hendrick barked at me again, in his heavy Dutch.

This time I ignored him. I was too tired.

Hendrick came out from behind the curtain. I turned my head away from him and looked slightly to the right. Straight into the eyes of John Kemble. I closed my eyes then, too embarrassed to look into those kind eyes, and hugged my arms again.

The exhibition hall was freezing. All the people were dressed in their outdoor clothing. Men were wearing greatcoats and waistcoats and cravats around their necks for warmth. Women wore chamois coats with satin linings, which reached down to their ankles.

"She's falling asleep," a woman screeched in a high-pitched voice. I pretended to keep my eyes closed, but I was peeping from underneath them, at the woman.

She was kneeling in front of the cage, peering up under my dress, her green eyes large and shocked. She had been staring up for at least five minutes. Pretending to tie her shoelaces, the woman sat on her haunches, her head bent sideways as she tried to get a better look from under the little cloth which covered my private parts under the dress. I opened my eyes and they looked straight into John Kemble's. I could see that he was very angry. I was angry too. I bit my lip and scowled down at the woman.

1810. Touched. Poked at. See woman peeping up under Saartjie's apron. 'The second man in uniform and the elegantly attired lady are both trying to sneak a peek at Saartjie's tablier. The man: "How odd nature is," while the woman, hoping to get a better look from below, crouches under pretence of tying her shoes. Meanwhile, the dog reminds us that we are all the same biological object under various attires.' [27]

Then someone poked a parasol through the metal bars of the cage and stabbed me in my soft flesh from behind. "Is this natural?" the voice asked stupidly.[28]

"Aargh!" I shouted. I could hold back my anger no longer. I shouted so suddenly that the green-eyed woman's husband, who was peering through the metal bars of the cage with an eye-glass, jumped back. He tripped over their dog, which yelped and jumped out of his way.

At that moment, I turned and hit down onto the parasol. The parasol fell with a loud clang into the cage.

"What a savage!" the woman shouted, stepping back and tripping over her wide skirts. But instead of falling into her husband's arms as she had expected, she stumbled back. Her husband, instead of helping her, stepped further out of her way. I thought good for you!

The commotion forced Hendrick Cezars to come out from behind his curtain. He ran around the cage to the woman.

"My sincerest apologies, madam," he murmured, offering her his hand, helping her up. Flustered, she pointed at me.

The parasol was lying inside the cage, on the little stage at my feet.

The crowd went silent. All eyes were fixed on the parasol. I stared at Hendrick, frozen in fear.

Hendrick took full advantage of the situation. With exaggerated care, he opened the low gate of the cage and pulled himself up onto the stage. As he came close to me, I stepped back. I thought that he was going to strike me, for he came towards me with a stick in his hand.[29]

With the stick out in front of him, Hendrick stepped forward. He made as if he was facing the gravest danger. He bent down, one hand behind him with the stick held high. With the other hand, he slowly reached for the parasol. He kept his eyes fixed on me, then stood up, holding the stick between us.

Not a sound came from the crowd.

I was mesmerised with fear. My eyes were glued to the stick. As Hendrick moved closer, I stepped back and felt the cold bars of the cage against my back. I could go no further.

"Stay!" Hendrick barked out at me in English. His voice boomed across the hall. He paused dramatically, as if I were an angry wild animal.

He quickly jumped back and out of the cage, slamming the gate shut.

Once outside the cage, he slowed down his movements again, like a magician exaggerating each careful move. He knew all eyes were on him as he pulled a metal chain out of the pocket of his coat. He fixed the chain in place and padlocked the gate.

The crowd clapped as he turned around. He bowed three times, his silly dark red wig (which he was wearing only since he came to England), shifting forward.

My knees gave in, and I sank to the floor. I cried without tears. My tears had dried up long ago.

"Stand up!" I heard him shout from behind the curtain where he had once more disappeared.

I jumped up and leaned against the side of the cage. I trembled. I felt lost and defeated.

"Poor creature. Poor, poor creature," I heard John Kemble murmur to himself.

Hendrick saw John Kemble and he came back from out of his curtain. "Please feel free to touch her, sir," he said.[30] The man ignored him.

Then John Kemble caught my eye. I could see the kindness in his face and I could not look away. I pulled myself away from the metal bars and turned my body squarely towards him. I looked straight at him this time. I patted my palms together, as we Khoi do when in front of someone we respect.

"Baba, Baba!"[31] I said.

"What did she say?" John Kemble asked Hendrick. "Does she call me her papa?"

"No, sir. She says you are a very fine man." He lied again.

"Upon my word," said John Kemble dryly. He was looking at me from the side, with his head at an angle. He looked pleased. "Upon my word, the lady does me infinite honour!" he said.

"Do touch her, sir, if you so wish," Hendrick said again. "It is without additional fee," he stressed.

John Kemble pulled back. "No, no!" he said. "Poor creature, no!"

I could see tears in his eyes as he turned away from me. "Now that was a sight which made me melancholy," he said to his friend as they turned to walk away from the cage. "I dare say, now, they ill-use that poor creature! Good God. How very shocking!" I heard him say.

And yet—not too long after that—the court believed Hendrick when he said I wanted to stay in England, that I wanted to be put on display, that I did not want to go back to see my family. All things which he and that doctor Alexander Dunlop made up between them, and forced me to say. All things which they wrote down and made me put my mark against. I was so scared of them that I agreed to repeat those lies to the men whom the court sent to speak with me personally. I said those things to them because I was afraid.

But the whole world believed Hendrick's lies.

As the rest of the people followed John Kemble out of the hall that night, I fainted. The day had been too long.

I woke up as Hendrick dimmed the lights. He returned to my cage. He unlocked the gate, stepped into the cage and pulled me roughly to my feet.

Slowly I came awake. I shivered, this time not from cold, but from fear and fever. My body was hot and felt dry. I could feel yet another boil in my groin. The boils had started developing a few days before. A small one, throbbing ones, big ones.

I stood up, confused and unhappy. I leaned against the metal bars as Hendrick walked away, leaving the gate of the cage open.

I closed my eyes, trying to understand what had gone wrong. My mind could not wrap itself around the change of events, try as I might. I could not figure it out.

It was not as if it had been my decision alone. It was a big decision. In our culture sending a woman away on a big ship to faraway lands was a big decision.

Frowning, not understanding, I moved out of the cage. Slowly, with difficulty, I climbed down from my platform of persecution, shivering with thirst and fever.

This was how most of my days went.

I bent to pick up the small bottle of brandy which Hendrick had left on the floor outside the cage. I shuffled forward, then stood still, threw my head back and drank from the bottle. The alcohol sent a coil of soothing heat down into my quivering insides and they went quiet.

Hendrick was sitting at a small table in the hallway, counting the money which had been taken at the door that day. He smiled at me as I walked out of the door. One of his very few smiles.

We did not have far to walk, but I struggled to keep up with Obi, the boy. I found it hard to lift one foot after the other. I struggled along, hugging my body inside the huge grey coat.

Nature Mother

The dream became worse after that. Still the same dream, always inside the laboratory of death inside the garden in Paris. But now there were all sorts of bodies and shapes around me.

If only I had taken notice, perhaps...but perhaps what?

There was nothing I could do about how things were going, for I was in a strange land, in the hands of people who had total control over me.

They made drawings of my body in the dream.

They cut open my private parts, like the healers did with snakes to get their poison out. They took my brain out. They took my back-passage out and put wax into it. My skull, upside down, stared at me, while the rest of my body stood without flesh in a box of glass with numbers on it, for many, many moons. Moons so far away that they fell off the earth and rolled away, and still I was standing there in the glass cage.

I could not understand life any longer. I still do not understand.

"Nature Mother gave me my body," I would say out loud into the darkness of my little room when I tried to make sense of it all. "Nature Mother gave us our bodies. When child was first born to woman."

"What do you know," I whispered to the evil spirits so they would leave me alone. "You know nothing. My ancestors trekked through the deserts after food when the earth went dry. The milk dried up and the young could not be fed. You don't know about how Nature Mother felt sorry for our young. They cried, hungry, they cried. They needs food. Children needs food. But sometimes, when there is no rain, women's breasts go dry."

"Then Nature Mother, because she knows everything and can see ahead in time and wanted her Great Race not to die, she put plenty of fat low on our bodies. But only on bodies of some special women. She gave us fat so that our young can have food and so that her race would survive."

I came awake with a start. I pushed my lips out. I pushed my chin up. I am a good person. I come from an honest nation. They won't let me think anything else.

My buttocks might not be a matter of pride to these people, but they are Nature Mother's gift to me and my people, and I accept them so.

The English People

Obi could read and write. He said that he went to one missionary Sunday school to learn how to do that.

I'd asked him not to tell anyone that I could speak English. His English was full of words from his home country which sometimes I could not understand.

"Aw, Sarkey!" he said to me one day when nobody was around "You understand everything. And all this time you made out like you don't understand."

"What is the number of the year now?" I whispered, for I could only measure time by the sun and the moon, nor by hot and cold times. And since I came to live in England I could not measure time because the sun did not stand in the same place in the sky. And in London, for very long days, the sun did not come out from behind the smoke, and the moon hid behind dark, heavy clouds.

"It is one thousand eight hundred and ten years," Obi's smile was much older than his 13 years. "And you have been in this country for three months," he said, because I had frowned. One thousand eight hundred and ten years meant nothing to me.

Obi told me that the English people were angry with Hendrick for putting me on show. He saw it in the newspapers, and sometimes he would bring the papers home. I could not read the papers, but I could see the pictures and they never really looked quite like me.

Obi showed me many papers, and I was surprised at how many people were complaining. "One man says it is enough to make the angels weep!" Obi said, holding up a newspaper and laughing. We thought it was very funny. We could not stop laughing. The ribbon which Obi tied around my waist every morning pulled into my flesh, and I had to put my finger under it because it felt like it would break, I laughed so much.

Another newspaper man wrote, and Obi read this out to me in his slow, concentrated way:

'The poor creature pointed to her throat and to her knees as if she felt pain in both, pleading with tears that he would not force her compliance. He declared that she was sulky, produced a long piece of bamboo, and shook it at her; she saw it, knew its power, and though ill, delayed no longer. While she was playing on a rude kind of guitar, a gentleman in the room chanced to laugh; the unhappy woman, ignorant of the cause, imagined herself to be the object of it, and as though the slightest addition to the woes of sickness, servitude and involuntary banishment from her native land was more than she could bear, her broken spirit was aroused for a moment, and she endeavoured to strike him with the musical instrument which she held; but the sight of the long bamboo, the knowledge of its pain, and the fear of incurring it again, calmed her. The master declared that she was wild as a beast, and the spectators agreed with him, forgetting that the language of ridicule is the same, and understood alike, in all

countries, and that not one of them could bear the subject of derision without an attempt to revenge the insult.'[32]

I could not understand everything when Obi read it to me, but what we knew was that what the man was saying was true.

"Is it true that they pay 2 shillings to go and see you?" Obi asked me. I shrugged. How was I supposed to know?

Zachary Macaulay[33]

The man with the big feet came to see Hendrick one afternoon. His name was Lord Macaulay.

I know because Obi told me. Obi also told me that Lord Macaulay had 12 children! I was shocked because in our culture we hardly ever have more than just a few children. We Khoi know how to make sure we have few children. The Dutch people also have many, many children. And the English.

I was sitting in my little room in the back of the house when Obi ran in, excited. "You must come and see who's here!" he said, his eyes big and excited.

"Sarkey, come on!" he pulled me by my hand, down the steps and through the kitchen. "It's Lord Macaulay."

"They are talking about you!" Obi said pushing me through the kitchen door into the passage.

"Who is he?" I asked, irritated, but also curious, for all I could see, through the open door, were the funny big feet of a man. Big bones were pushing through his shoes on each side where his big toes were.

"He is a well-known abolitionist."

"What's a abolisinis?" I asked, because it sounded like people living in sin, as the missionaries used to say is not allowed by their god.

"He is a very important somebody. He works for the African Association. They make sure that slaves are made free. Like me!" he said proudly. I said nothing. I could not see how he could be free, when he was still working so many long hours and was being treated worse than me.

We went to stand under the stairs. We could hear the voices from the sitting room clearly. Some of what was said I could not understand, but Obi explained everything to me afterwards.

"Where does the female come from?" Macaulay was saying.

"I brought her from the interior of the Cape of Good Hope down to Cape Town." It was Hendrick's voice.

"Did the Governor of the Cape give you permission to bring the female to this country?"

"Yes, I was given permission."

"The liar!" I muttered in my own language, and Obi gave me a bad look.

Now I understood why they had taken me to Saldanha Bay to get on the ship. It was because he had no permission. And that is why he kept me away from everyone on the ship, over the whole journey. I had spent all that time sleeping between bags of corn and nobody was allowed to come and see me. And I was sneaked off the ship!

"I'm surprised," Lord Macaulay said. "Did Lord Caledon, the Governor at the Cape give permission for her to be brought to England?"

"Yes." I could hear that Hendrick was getting angry.

"Are you sure?"

"Of course I'm sure, sir!"

"Is the permission in writing?"

"Yes, it is."

"Are you quite sure that Lord Caledon knows that the woman was to be brought to this country to be exhibited?"

"Oh! Yes. Yes!"

"May I please see the written permission given by Lord Caledon?"

I heard after the court case that Lord Macaulay knew Lord Caledon personally. It was in the papers that Lord Macaulay even knew Lord Caledon's handwriting, that is why he wanted to see the letter of permission.[34]

Hendrick was quiet.

"I would like to see Lord Caledon's written permission, please. I would like to see where he signed that the woman could be brought to England to be exhibited."

"Won't you believe my word, sir! I have already told you that he has signed it!"

"I do not believe you Mr Cezars. I do not believe your pronouncement of how you came possessed of the woman. I believe your story to be a complete fake." Lord Macaulay now sounded angry.

"I do not care what you believe, sir," Hendrick answered. "The woman was the servant of a friend of Lord Caledon's. Lord Caledon permitted her to come from the Cape of Good Hope. He is well apprised of the purpose for which she came."

"Why do you not show me Lord Caledon's permission which you say is in writing?"

"I have already told you that he has signed it. I shall give you no further satisfaction or conversation!"

We heard the front door open and then there was silence, and we went into the kitchen, so that Obi could explain everything to me.

This is the transcript of a letter received by the Supreme Court, London, the next year:[35]

From Earl of Caledon
Castle of the Cape of Good Hope
March 1811

Your Lordship,

It having been stated in a recent trial before Lord Ellenborough that a female Hottentot had been carried out of this colony with my knowledge and consent, it is due to the high situation I have the honour to hold, for me to acquaint Your Lordship that I was wholly ignorant of the transaction until long after her departure and that she never did apply for or receive permission to leave the colony.

Honourably Yours
Alexander du Pré, Earl of Caledon[36]

Lies, Lies, Lies[37]

Later that night Obi came to call me again.

"The doctor and Hendrick want to see you!" He stumbled over his words when he was in a hurry to be a good slave.

The big room was very cold that night. Nobody had lit the fire. The doctor was sitting staring out of the big window, ignoring me when I came into the room. I went to stand behind the big chair on the other side. Hendrick was facing me, a scowl on his face.

They did not speak with me, just sat there in silence, ignoring me for a few minutes and I wanted to run out of that room. I wanted to run away, because my heart was telling me that things are going to be bad, that they were going to tell me bad things.

I was very afraid of them.

"Do you like to be in England?" Hendrick asked at last, staring up at me with blood-shot eyes.

"Yes." I did like being in a country where people care about each other, like they care about me.

"Do you want to go home?"

"Yes." Of course I wanted to go home. What a silly question.

"That is not what you told me the other day," Hendrick said. I gasped. What was he talking about!

"You said you wanted to stay in this country, that you were not missing your family."

"I never said that!"[38] I forgot myself and raised my voice. Hendrick jumped up and came to stand right in front of me. Scared, I stepped back. I could see that his temper was rising.

"What is she saying?" said the doctor Dunlop in English, for he could not understand what Hendrick and I were saying in Dutch.

"She is being stubborn," Hendrick said, not taking his eyes off my face.

"You will tell them you do not want to go back to your country, you understand? You will tell them you do not miss your family!" This, again in Dutch.

Then he told me they would leave me to die in England if I did not do what they said.

I was scared. What could I do?

"Give her the contract," Dunlop said impatiently. Hendrick lifted a sheet of paper from the table and gave me a pen.

"Put your mark here," he ordered. I did.

"And when they come, don't forget to tell them that you are waiting for your money, that you are going to stay here for six years and then you will take your money back with you."

I looked up at the man with hatred. I looked over at the doctor. Doctor Alexander Dunlop was staring at the floor. He would not look up at me.

"But…"

"What?" Hendrick barked.

"You said two years..."[39] I had to say it, even though I was very scared.

"I said six years!"[40] he said, shaking his fist at me. "Get out of the room," he ordered, and I obeyed.

I went to my room to sit on my tin trunk under the small window. I could just see through the little window, which was very dirty. I could not see anything, no trees, no veld, no animals, no sea. Just the red brick wall of the house next door.

A tired-looking blanket was lying under the window, crying out for the sun, dirty and grey. I hoped that I would not also end up looking like that. Already my skin was starting to shrink and go bloodless in its need for the sun.

I kicked the tangled woollen blanket with its bad luck out of my way and took my little leather pouch out of my trunk. I opened the pouch and pinched some tobacco between my thumb and finger. I turned my hand over and gently crunched the rough tobacco into a soft powder. I closed my eyes, and pushed down onto one nostril and breathed the tobacco powder deep into the other one.

I did this a few times until all the powder was gone, until my body relaxed against the cold and my thoughts flew home.

I must be patient. Tata had taught me to be patient. I must remember that my family is depending on me to take the money back to them. I must be like my ancestor, Herry[41], who travelled on big ships to far away countries, speaking many languages. He came home and everyone knew him. Still now, all our fathers and grandfathers boast about how famous Herry was.

"Herry, the interpreter," they would say to us. "Do not forget how all the white people admired him, because he could speak many languages and helped them to understand our people," they would repeat the story to us.

I must be like Herry, who took the money he earned in the faraway lands back to his people.

And Krotoa,[42] called Eva, who was a great ancestor of mine. Krotoa was married to a very important doctor and she lived like a princess in the home of the important Dutch Governor, *Meneer*[43] Van Riebeek. She was much admired by all young girls, because she became a very important somebody in the high places in Cape Town.

I must remember them and be like them.

I fell asleep with good thoughts, which chased the evil ghosts away when they tried to pull my lips back, tried to pinch my skin as if looking for nits on the body of an ape. Smoke floated over them and took them away.

Smoke which smelt of pine, of burnt lavender. It filled my dream and took me out of my little room in the back of the big house in York Street,[44] London, back home. It lingered there in my family hut eight thousand miles away, blanking out my mind with good thoughts.

I was a little girl again, sitting on the floor between Tata's legs in front of the fire. I heard Tata's quiet voice through the sound of soft rain outside and through the moaning of the cattle and the shuffling of their bodies in the centre of the *kraal*. And the smell of cow-dung fused in my head with memories of love.

"Long ago, the First Man came out of the earth's great womb," Tata's soft voice held me close, "he came out of the earth's womb followed by all the animals. Our people were the first. Khoikhoi. First People. Men of Men."

The pounding in my head the next morning at first felt like the far away beat of a drum, a wedding invitation across the veld,[45] in time to the rhythm of my heart.

Then Obi woke me up with breakfast of bread and sausage—strange, unpleasant food, and my heart started racing again.

Suddenly the light disappeared from the little window as the sun hid its face from my world and shadows crept back, heavy with the fear of my sweat.

Bigger than yesterday, fear came and consumed my soul as I realised that today was the day when I would have to tell all those lies.

Questions, Questions, Questions

"The Court told us to come and speak with you," the man said.

There were too many men there in the room with me, the room at the front of the house.

"My name is Peter van Wageninge. I work with Lord Macaulay," he said. "And this is Mr James Templar, the Coroner of the Court," pointing to a very tall man with a thin face and long fingers. He introduced the other two men as a *Meneer* Solly and a *Meneer* Moojen. "They can speak Dutch too and they will help everyone understand," he said with a smile, looking at the *Meneer* Coroner.

He also introduced the other two important men from the court, but I can't remember all their serious English names.

"Do you know what a court is, Saartjie?" he asked.

I nodded. He spoke Dutch the way I speak it. That is why he could say my Dutch name properly.

I was feeling really bad. I knew that I was going to have to tell lies to this man, whom I recognised. *Meneer* Van Wageninge. I liked him. I did not want to tell lies.

I remembered the day before, when he had come to the exhibition. He had tried to speak with me.

But every time he had tried to talk with me, Hendrick had come out and would not leave us alone, so I had not answered him, although I had wanted to. Hendrick knew I could understand what *Meneer* Van Wageninge was trying to say to me, because he spoke to me in Dutch.

"Where do you come from?" he had asked, "Do you have any relations? Do you have any children? Are you happy? Are you comfortable here? Do you want to go home?"

He had asked all those questions, but I could not answer them. I had stood sighing, many times, but I could not reply. I had kept my head down, afraid that if I met his eye I would start to cry. So I had kept quiet because Hendrick was there.[46]

Now *Meneer* Van Wageninge was back. His face had the same permanent frown of concern on it, as it did when he came to see me at the show.

Now I still cannot answer his questions honestly. This is very bad. When in our custom we hold counsel, and all the adults are there, and everyone is solemn, you show respect. In our custom, you never told a lie to your Kaptein in counsel. And the English court is the same thing.

And I think I remembered the *Meneer* Coroner but can't be sure. I think it was to him that Hendrick said she's always sulky when company is there, when the *Meneer* told him to stop being so unkind to me. I remember that Hendrick wanted me to play on my r*amkie* that day. I was feeling too ill, too tired. I pointed to my throat and to my knees. I could not stop crying. But Hendrick wanted to hit me. And then a man laughed and I became very angry, so I lifted my *ramkie* to Hendrick. That was the day that Hendrick called me a 'wild beast', in front of all those people, that day, and they agreed with him. And the *Meneer* had walked away.

"This is Mr Babington," *Meneer* Van Wageninge's voice came to me over my thoughts. "And of course, you know Dr

Alexander Dunlop." I looked at all the other men. I did not look at the doctor. I did not want him to be there.

If the doctor had not been there, I would, perhaps, have had the courage to tell the truth, not to say what he and Hendrick had told me to say. But because the doctor was there I had to do what they had told me to say.

"We are grateful to Doctor Dunlop for attending,"[47] said *Meneer* Van Wageninge. That is when my spirit started to die, for it knew that my whole life could have been different if that doctor had not been there, the same man who had threatened me.

"I must explain to you what has happened," *Meneer* Van Wageninge was saying. "I work for the African Association. Do you know who they are, Saartjie?" I nodded. Obi had explained to me that they work to set slaves free.

"The African Association has asked the court to set you free," he said. My heart leaped. Just for a moment some light came through the cracks of my heartbreak. Then it disappeared again.

"The court said that we must ask you some questions," one of the other men said. He was very ugly, with big teeth which were wide apart, and he talked with spit at the sides of his lips. "I and my colleague here," pointing to the fifth man, "are Examiners of the Court. The court wants to order that you be returned to your country."

"You need to explain to her what *habeas corpus* is," he said to *Meneer* Van Wageninge.

"Ja. The court will tell them to stop the exhibition, to produce your body to the court, so the court can see if you are safe."

"Is it true that Hendrick Cezars is no longer your master? He told the court the other day that he is no longer your master, because the people complained too much."

ANOTHER LIE my brain shouted and I gasped.

"Bring her some water," the *Meneer* said to Obi, who was listening in the corner, trying to protect me as he always did. They thought I was thirsty.

"Last Saturday they held a special court for you," he explained. "On Tuesday of next week, the court will hear your answers. Do you know what the date that will be, Saartjie?" I shook my head.

"It will be the 27th of November 1810 next Tuesday, the day when the court will give an order about you."

"But the court will not let you go unless you say that you want to go back to your people. They said you must say this of your own free will. You must choose where you want to go and with whom you want to go."

I said nothing. I knew I could not say anything because Hendrick and the doctor would never let me go. The doctor was staring at me, and fear came out in streams of sweat which ran down over my forehead, came out under my arms and ran down between my breasts and my back.

"Who brought you to England, Saartjie?"

"Hendrick Cezars, *meneer*."

"Did he take you to get permission from the Governor at the Cape?" I nodded, afraid to say that this had never happened. I glanced at the doctor, who nodded and smiled.

"Did you sign an agreement?" I nodded.[48]

"Are you going to get some money?"

"Yes, I am getting half of the money."

"What is the date of the agreement?"

"I don't know."[49] I had the paper in my hand. The doctor had given it to me to give to them that morning. Hendrick was not there that morning.

"It is dated 29th October 1810, but it says here the agreement started on 20th March 1810. I do not understand," the other *Meneer* said.

He looked up at me.

"Can you read?"

"No."

"Can you write?"

"No."

He looked at the paper. "It says here you will 'allow yourself to be viewed by the public of Ireland and England just as you are.' Is that true?" I did not reply.

"Do you mind being seen, being viewed like that?" he asked, his voice kind and concerned. I did not reply, I was feeling too ashamed.

"Do they treat you kindly?" I nodded.

"Do you have complaints to make?" I shook my head.

"Are you happy?"

"Yes." Again I lied!

"Do you want to go back to your own country?" I looked up at the two men. I could not believe that anyone could ask me such a question. I opened my mouth to say this, then I glanced at the doctor, who was staring very hard at me. I heard Hendrick's gruff voice in my head, "You must tell them you don't want to go back to Cape Town, else Doctor Dunlop and I will leave you and there will be nobody to look after you and you will starve to death."

"No, I do not want to go back to my country," I said.

"What did you say?" the first *Meneer* asked, for I had spoken so softly he could not hear me. My eyes filled with tears and I had to keep my head down for many minutes. Then I lifted my eyes.

"Stay here." My throat would not let my voice come past. It was blocked with frozen anguish and tears.

"Do you have money?"

"Yes, they give money."

"What do you do that is nice?" and I looked at Obi who smiled at me, before I answered, "I go for a coach ride every Sunday.[50] I do go with Obi." That was true. I loved going in the coach with Obi through the gardens in London, past the big church called St Paul's and past the big clock called Big Ben and past the palace where the English king lives. Once, when the coachman stopped off, we were allowed to go to Newgate prison, but they were not hanging anyone there that day and I was glad, because I do not like to see people being killed.

"Where is your father, your mother?"

"My mother died when I was two years old. My father was killed some time ago."

"Do you have any children?"

"No."

"Did you have a baby?"

"Yes."

"Did your baby die?"

"Yes."

"Who is the father of your baby?"

"Paddy."[51]

"Who is Paddy?"

"He is a soldier."

"How old are you?"

I was going to say I did not know, but then I remembered Obi saying to me that they said in one of the newspapers that I was twenty two years old.

"Twenty two," I answered.

"How long were you at the Cape?"

"About three winters and three summers."

"For how long are you staying in this country?"

"Two…" and then, because the doctor Dunlop cleared his throat, I lied, "…six years," I lied, catching his eye.

"Do you have any other family in the Cape?"

"Yes."

"Who are they?"

"Two brothers and three sisters."

"Do you want to go back to them?"

This time I could not answer. I just dropped my head and cried inside. That was one lie I could not say again.

"The unfortunate woman sealed her own destiny," I heard *Meneer* Van Wageninge say as they gathered up their papers.[52]

I ran out of the door ahead of them, into my little room, threw myself down on my *kaross* and bit my lips until blood seeped through them and mingled with my tears as the sobs tore my chest apart.

Final Departure

For a short time, after that day, people still came to see me. But it was just for a few moons that I stood there, every morning leaving my soul behind me in the little room in York Street.

Soon the crowds disappeared, and people stopped coming.

And Hendrick changed his name.

He had to change his name, I thought, because they must have found out about his lies. When I said this to Obi, he said to me, in the serious way of young men, "He is waiting to see how he can make more money out of you. I hope he does not take you far away from me, Sarkey."

And this is exactly what Hendrick did. Now called Henry Taylor, he took me out of London on coaches and put me in taverns to sleep and entertain people. I cannot count the many journeys we made through the country called England.

I spent my time in the taverns at night. I was given brandy to drink, because by now I did not care. For three summers and winters we travelled around so.

I missed Obi. I missed the only friend I had made in that whole country. They did not even give me a chance to say goodbye to him, for we left London late one night and never went back.

By now, I could understand the English language much better, and I could speak with people. I could laugh with people, especially when they bought me something to drink in the taverns. I could play cards with them.

But NEVER did I go and sleep with any man. I know that this is what people were saying about me, because I heard them speak. They spoke openly, because they thought that I could not understand them. They spoke on the streets when I walked past them. They spoke about me when I sat in a garden. They spoke about me in the taverns.

They said I was doing things with men. I never answered, for I have learnt that they would always regard me as something not normal, a freak. I have learnt that freaks do not get allowed a normal life.

So I did not answer them.

But one evening it became almost too much for me. How I managed to keep silent I cannot remember.

I was sitting on a bench by the seaside. It was in a place called Bath. I was enjoying the setting sun. I always wore a big cloak when I went out, because I did not want people to recognise me.

There were two men sitting behind me, on the other side of the tree. My back was turned to them. I do not think they saw me.

"I'm going to see Hottentot Venus," the first man said.

"Oh! You will find it very interesting," his friend answered. They spoke in high English, and some of the words were too high for me. But I knew when they said Hottentot Venus that they were speaking about me, so I kept listening.

"Is it true that the Hottentot women have long flaps growing out by their genitals?" the first man asked.

"I've read up about them," his friend answered. He sounded quite serious. "The people are called KhoiKhoi. I believe they call themselves Quaei-Quaei, which means small people of the apron. They always wear a little apron in front."

"Actually, I know about their genital flaps. I've read about that too."

"Is it true that once you've had sex with a black woman, you never want to go with another woman again?"

"How must I know?" his friend said.

"Well, I am a scientist and I know that the books have recorded the size of the Hottentot's clitoris for years. And I quote, 'The bigger the clitoris in a woman, the more lustful they are.' That is why their long vaginal side walls are called curtains of shame," he ended, clearing his throat. He sounded more embarrassed than me. I stopped myself from jumping up and running away. I did not want to draw attention to myself.

What I did know was that they, as all the men did who came to see me, were thinking about me in the wrong way.

"Steatopygia," I heard the voice of the man of science. Another big science word.

"What?"

"Steatopygia," he repeated. "An accumulation of fat around the behinds of some people. It is found especially in the South African aborigines. Some scientists believe that it has the same function as the fat tails of the sheep which the Hottentots inherited from the Arabs. Like the fat of the *dromedary*, the one-humped camel. I believe it is so that they can move faster."

"Is the fat needed for running, then?" his friend must have bent his head down, because I found it hard to hear him.

"The fat on the women helps them to feed their babies in the desert. It turns into water." Now that I knew too.

"What about the men, then? If the women's fat is for feeding the young, why do the men have these enormous, massive, you-know-what's?"

Silence. They were thinking very deeply about nonsense.

"Did you know that Hotnot men have just one ball?" the conversation started up again.

"*Scrotum.*"

"Well, you know what I mean. My friend says they are not shy. They will lift up their cloaks and show you if you ask them. My friend spent some time in the Cape of Good Hope, so he should know."

"*Monorchids.* They are called that because they have just one testicle. It is the medical term for having one testicle."

His friend laughed. "Do they cut the ball off?"

"No, they pull them up so that they can run faster. It also helps them with birth control. They always have only a few babies."

Now that was news to me. They got up and walked away, and left me with lots to think about. They seem to know more about my own people than I ever did, I thought as the sun went down over the sea at Bath.

Soon after that we left England. Hendrick (sorry, Henry Taylor) put me on a little boat and took me to a country called France.

But he could not get me there without papers. This I knew, because I knew how hard it was for him to get me out of one country to another. He could not get me out of yet another country hidden in another ship. He had to get me a paper with my name on it. And it had to show an English name.

So he worked out a very clever plan.

It was a very cold morning, deep in the winter, when I was taken to one of the churches. We travelled very far to get to that church. It was far from the seaside. It was a coach which went to Manchester, on a long road, for one day and a night we slept on the coach.

There I met a very happy man. He was short, almost my size, and I am very short. He had big, bushy eyebrows and spoke in funny English. His name was Reverend Brookes.

He took me into his church, an empty, big building, with high windows with pictures in them. He put water on my head and said, "I baptize[53] you in the name of the Father, the Son and the Holy Ghost."

The brandy in my head made me laugh, it was all very funny.

That was the last silly thing that happened to me in the land of England.

The other thing was not silly. It was sad. I want to forget about it.

Hendrick took me to see the doctor Dunlop.

We travelled again by coach for two days and a night, back to the sea. It was a bright day, the sun was shining and the sea birds were flying about like they do in Cape Town when the wind sometimes leaves them alone to enjoy themselves.

"We must pay our last respects," Hendrick said, and for the first time, and for the last time, in that England, I agreed with him.

We walked up a long road to a small house on a dirty street in a town called Portsmouth. A thin slave woman with spindly legs opened the door, fear in her eyes. The house was very dark. All windows and curtains were closed, and the house smelt of pee and boiled cabbage.

I did not recognise the doctor. He lay in his bed, on his back in a little back room, his mouth open, his eyes closed. He looked like a sad *snoek*—as the Dutch call the big fish which we catch in the warm seas in Cape Town—when they know they are going to die.

He had the same cold, bloodless, wet look. His chest was quiet for a long time, then it heaved. He gasped and his chest went still again, no breathing.

I walked to his bed with my head bowed and the palms of my hands together in respect for the dying man. The coldness of death was clinging to my skin under the big cloak I was wearing, creeping with cold legs like frightened baby lizards up my spine, making the hairs stand up.

I remembered that the doctor Dunlop was the one who could have saved my baby, if only I had allowed Paddy to take Themba to the Slave Lodge hospital that day, when he wanted to do that. The man in front of me would have saved my baby, for that was his job, even if he did not know how to be a good person in ordinary life. I felt sorry for him, for myself. I crossed his room of death and walked out of his life with much sadness in my heart.

Soon after that I left with Henry Taylor on a ship and crossed another sea, to another country.

Paris[54]

I lived right inside Paris. I did not need to walk far to go and do my six hours standing. Sometimes, when there were many people, the animal keeper[55] made me stand for 12 hours. I learnt how to stand in my sleep. The brandy helped me to do that.

I lived on top of the exhibition hall. I soon learnt that the address was *15 rue Neuve des Petits Champs* in Paris, overlooking the Palais Royal gardens.

The dreams started to come up again. But I was drinking lots of brandy and I did not care.

The evil spirits were always lingering in the bottom of my stomach, sitting in the bowl with my woman parts, throbbing, waiting to come up. They mixed there with the pains which never went away. They fought with the boils which pinched and punched me and sent their angry fever cursing through my veins.

I was drinking lots of brandy and I did not care.

Paddy never came to look for me. But I did not care.

The longing for my family had turned my heart into a heavy stone which sat in my chest hardened by grief. All my bones were heavy and slow. My soul never saw the sun again in that lovely city called Paris, because I would not let it come out. If I was never going to see my family again, I did not want to go on living.

In Paris I was sold. SOLD to an ugly man called Reaux. A dirty Frenchman who kept animals.

In Paris, I became an animal and I want to forget all about that.

So I drink the brandy which they give me. I drink because they do not give me much food. I drink to stop the pain from burning my body up. I drink to keep alive.

They made drawings of me yesterday. The drawings were different this time. They did not look like the stupid drawings which poked fun at me.

I dressed up specially for the drawings. I wore my *kaross*. I took my *ramkie* with me and put on all my trinkets. I wore my little loin cloth. I wanted them to see how our people looked. I sang for them, but they did not seem to want that.

The main man of science called the men behind a tree, and they talked with each other. Then they came back to me. There was a man there who could speak Dutch and he spoke with me.

"The doctors would like you to take your clothes off," he said, his eyes looking down.

"What?"

"They say will you please take your clothes off."

"No." I turned away from him and brought my lips together and folded my arms. I was not going to do that.

He walked around me and started pleading, "Please do as they ask, *juffrou*," he said politely. They know when to call you Miss when they want something out of you. "Please try to understand. This is for science. They want to make drawings of your people as they are." Those words again, 'as you are', the same words they had written into their agreement in England.

I did not bother to open my eyes. And I kept my mind shut, too, away from those people as I'd learnt to do. I just shook my head and stood there with my eyes closed as if I was sleeping.

They went away again. I could hear them speak. They spoke in French. I could understand a bit of French, but I could not understand what they were saying, because they were speaking in words of science.

"We will not be able to prove or disprove the *sinus pudoris*,"[56] one of them said.

"Absolutely. It will be a waste of time and money," another said.

"How will we be able to prove that they are a different species? We cannot, as scientists, perpetuate sailors' stories of the existence of the lengthened *labia minora.*"

"We do know that the Hottentot women have this *tablier*. It has been recorded for many years, for example by the great explorer Captain Cook. But it has never been replicated in the flesh. We owe it to science to record the famous apron…"

One of the other doctors came back. Thinking I could not see him, he tried to look under my loin cloth. He bent his long body in ridiculous ways to see, kneeling, then almost lying on the floor of the stage in front of me, trying to look up while holding his eyeglass in place. His beard scraped on the floor of the stage. I simply turned and he had to start all over again. Silly man.

This time the man who could speak Dutch came back with the doctor of science. His name was Doctor Cuvier.

Doctor Cuvier was very polite to me. Through the Dutch man he asked me to go with him to his rooms. He allowed me to put my *kaross* back on and walked politely next to me, not speaking. He took me up the steps of the Natural History Museum, to the upper floor.

I had a big shock when we got to his front door. Outside the door there were jars that looked like big bells, with funny, green feet and body parts in it. The glass of the jars was dirty and the liquid inside just as dirty, but there was no question: they were the parts of other people's bodies.

Just like in my dream!

I was shocked.

Once inside he asked me to sit in one of the comfortable chairs and went to a cupboard in the corner and brought back a big glass for me and two small ones for himself and the Dutch man, with brandy. The brandy was very welcome. It soon made my head feel comfortable, and it sent the evil spirits, boils and fevers to rest.

The doctor spoke with me through the interpreter for some time. He asked many questions, which I answered. He asked me about my family, about Cape Town, about the mountain which rises out of the sea and looks like a table. I told him about the cloud which settles on the table when the wind blows a certain way, how the cloud looks like a tablecloth falling over a real table.

I told him about the place where the two seas come together, the cold sea and the hot one.

"Ah, you mean the Indian ocean and the Atlantic Ocean!" he said through the interpreter, fascinated. He made me feel important. We were having a real conversation.

And all the while he kept filling my glass up with the wonderful brandy, which loosened my tongue and made me forget how sad my life was. Then he explained to me how important it is that they do drawings of me without my clothes on.

"Many people in the world," he explained through the interpreter, "look different from each other. Like you and me." I giggled, because it was true, except that he was just as small as I was and was also quite fat. But our skins were different.

"It is important for us to show how different your people are."

It was his next remark which made me agree. "We scientists think that your people are the First Race," he said, and I remembered that Tata had said the same thing. "This is why it is important that the whole world should see what your bodies look like, to show how people's bodies have changed." I nodded. I could see what he was saying.

"Will you allow them to make drawings of you with only your little apron in front?" he asked politely.

"Ja," I said to the Dutch interpreter with a smile, and I took another sip of brandy.

"And,"—and the doctor paused, giving me a very nice smile, "and will you, just for a very short time, drop your loin cloth so that they can do a quick picture of you without it on?"

Before I could answer, he said, "I promise that only the artists will be there. They do this all the time for science; they have no bad thoughts." When he said that, I understood.

"Ja *meneer*," I said, this time smiling, for the brandy had done its job and I was feeling good.

They took me back to the garden, into the Jardin des Plantes. He asked me to step back onto the platform and gave me a chair to rest my arm on. I watched the artists with their big books and small sketch books and eyeglasses.

They let me stand there for hours, while they did drawings of me.

When the doctor scientist Cuvier came back to me to ask me to drop my little loin cloth for a short while, I did it.

Nakedness is something beautiful. Our children are allowed to be naked. Our women and our men are allowed to be naked on top. But showing all your nakedness to other people is the worst shame there is. This I knew since I became a woman. It was part of my instruction when I became a woman. I had let myself and my people down.

The drink helped to soften the shame, but I was no longer proud to be a woman.

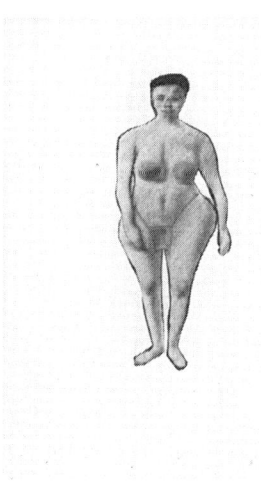

A drawing of Saartjie in the Jardin des Plantes (also known as Jardin du Rois), Paris.

What was Saartjie like? Cuvier,[57] the doctor who did the autopsy on Saartjie, described her as intelligent, 'with general proportions that would not lead connoisseurs to frown,' possessing and excellent memory, and spoke Dutch rather well and had some command of English. He admitted that her shoulders, back and chest 'had grace' and spoke of her charming hand. Yet he compared her to an orangutan![58] She was modest in nature. She had refused to remove her little apron when the above picture was drawn, according to Stephen Jay Gould (see Further Reading below).

On Becoming a Woman

The day I became a woman was the last day, ever, that I would go out hunting with the men.

It was a dreamy day, a deeply exciting day. We walked along the river, the Gamtoos river,[59] my favourite animal. Gamtoos. Water. Water always did something to me, stirred me inside, especially when it moved so slowly, lazily, throwing silver sparks up at the sun. With its very big torso, Gamtoos moved like an ancient animal. It called me.

Inside me my womanhood was responding, awakening. Strange, confusing desires and thoughts that were being awoken and heated by the African sun.

Bhuti was walking in front of me, naked. Only five years old, and no mother to look after him, my poor brother, I thought. He was carrying a dead rabbit by its hind legs. I noticed his young body, how his legs were spread wide. Taut muscles, straining in concentration, all his senses alert.

"Tata!" Bhuti shouted to our father sitting on a rock, doing men's work. Tata did not look up, and I wanted to scream at Bhuti to leave him alone. Tata was just about to push a short reed into the small bone he was holding. I watched to make sure he did not push it into his finger, smeared as it was with snake poison. I could only relax when he had put the reed and its poisoned head away safely.

It was after we had eaten the rabbit, put out the fire and drunk cool water from the river that I knew things were changing.

A strange wetness came between my legs. My inner thighs were slipping against each other.

"Heitsi Eibib," I mumbled as my sister does when things went wrong. Tata was not looking at me. He was smoking his pipe, his back towards me, so I looked down between my legs. I slipped a finger there and it came away covered in a thick, dark liquid.

Something big was happening. I smelt the liquid, which looked like mud. It had a strange, yet familiar, smell. I wiped my hand on my leg and it left behind a smear of blood. My heart skipped a beat. I knew then where the blood was coming from. I was frightened.

The blood started running down freely between my legs and I panicked. I was afraid that I would die like the sheep died when their throats are cut, and their blood is caught in bowls.

I did not want to die.

'*Heitsi-Eibib is punishing me,*' I thought. Because I had laughed at Tata. Through my fear I felt guilty. Heitsi-Eibib, the great-grandfather of the Khoi, would not have thought it funny. While I was laughing at Tata, Heitsi-Eibib had been looking at me from where he stood, the dawn-tree amongst the other trees. He had heard me laugh. Tata had looked so silly, opening and closing his jackal-skin wallet about three times, because he kept forgetting things. Even now, thinking about it, I felt like laughing again.

"Thandi!" Tata called as he slapped an old cow on her rump. The cow, just about to collapse into the ground, tried to straighten her bent legs in a comical way. I laughed again. At 13 everything in the world can be funny, even when you are very frightened.

"Thandi!" I heard him call again, and opened my eyes. The dream and the cow vanished, mooing, changing her mind, running out of the *kraal*.

Tata and Bhuti had come back for me. They were standing above me, staring at me. In my half-awake state I had moved, and folded my knees up. Blood was running down my lower thigh onto the soft earth.

I watched Tata's eyes as he saw this, with a frown on his face, and my head throbbed with shame.

!Habab[60]

Eight days later I sat alone, again by the riverbank.

This was my special day, my day of celebration. I had come through the last seven days of seclusion. I sat looking at my reflection in the water, at the way my breasts cupped up. My body trembled with excitement.

That morning the old woman had rubbed my body, first with the blood of the sheep which Tata had killed, then with its soft entrails, then with its fat. Lastly, I had ground the specially-chosen earth, ochre, into a soft powder, and had gently spread this over my body.

The yellow and red pigments of the ochre shone with a lovely orange glow on my brown skin. It looked like thousands of glittering quarts fragments.

I hummed softly with joy, a lullaby which the old lady had taught me while I was in seclusion. Then I switched to a love song and started singing out loud, and the bees buzzed, and the toads croaked in harmony. While I sang, I ran my hands down along the sides of my arms and legs, loving their softness. It felt really good when I ran my hands ever so lightly over my skin, not allowing my palms to make much contact. I was delirious with happiness.

My singing turned louder. A boastful song of the strength of women and of male jealousy. My voice rose and I sang of the obedience of men. Most of all, I loved the chorus urging the men to war. I sang that over and over again.

Suddenly I saw a face peep out from behind a rock. I jumped up, shocked, for I was naked. I just had time to see the side of a man's face, which disappeared behind the rock as soon as I saw him. I stood dead still, my heart pounding. My thigh muscles were quivering and pulling on my calves so tight was my body. I forced my body to stay still. I waited. My heart pounded in my chest.

Then from behind the rock came a very soft laugh and I knew who it was. Before he came out from behind the rock, he gave a soft whistle and followed this with a light song, in a strong, good voice. His voice was filled with laughter:

> *"You look like the girl of the Early Race*
> *Till the Milky Way smiled and threw*
> *Its wood ashes all over her*
> *You are so beautiful."*

It was Solkar. He appeared smiling, holding his hands up as if pleading for forgiveness, smooth, thick black eyebrows held up in half-moons. We both knew that he was doing wrong. Men were not allowed anywhere near a girl before her *!Habab* ceremony was over.

I knew that Solkar was going to come to my ceremony. He was the son of the Kaptein, and must have been on his way when he saw me.

I covered myself with my hands, and I stood still, too excited to move, good manners forgotten, as he walked towards me. He was carrying his little royal stool, a sign of his wealth and his royal blood. The dark cord which was woven into the seat of the stool rubbed against his well-oiled thighs under a spotted leopard skin loincloth. It matched the ivory bracelet on his upper arm and his ivory neckband.

I was overjoyed to see him.

Then I saw the women and panic pushed up into my throat.

We're going to be found out! I rolled my eyes because I could see them over his shoulder and Solkar had not seen them. His senses as sharp as those of a young tiger, Solkar jumped behind the rock again, out of sight. But not before he had shown me a necklace he was holding closely in his hand.

My older sister, Bithathe, walked towards me and with the old lady, my Master of Ceremonies, followed by the other women. They were there for my final instruction before they took me back to the *kraal* before the party began.

My eye caught Solkar again peeping from behind the women, and I had to hide a smile. Knowing nobody else was looking, Solkar immediately took advantage. With a broad smile over even white teeth, he held up a finger to his full, soft lips. Eyes dancing, he pretended to frown, then shrugged his shoulders in a plea for silence, and once more disappeared behind the rock.

I wanted to crash with laughter, but I had to keep a straight face, for the instructions were starting.

"Your special room is ready for you, Thandi," Bithathe said softly in my ear as her hand touched my arm in greeting. I was only half listening for I had heard Solkar walking away through the bush in the other direction.

"We put a special mat there in the room for you," Bithathe continued, our mother tongue lifting her deep voice with its clicks of silver.

Bithathe had to make all the arrangements in place of our mama. Mama had died when I was very young. Bithathe became the ruler of the household since then. She was feared by all, even by Tata. Since Mama died, Tata and my brothers had to obey Bithathe, as ruler of the house.

Then the old lady took over. She had come to give me my final instruction.

"*Molo mntwan'am!*" She called me her child. "*Molo makhulu!*" I replied, calling her grandmother, for she was of my grandmother's generation.

Spitting into the sand, she looked at me with her kind smile, knowledge lighting up her sun-creased face. She led the group instruction and the other women, one by one, took up their turn.

"Remember, your name is Thandi," she started, eyes twinkling. "Thandi is a good name, a strong name. One day you will have a husband. Your husband will have no say inside your hut. In the hut, you are the top ruler. Outside the hut, you listen to your husband."

Only one husband, she emphasised, looking around at all the other women, wagging her finger, eyes stern. Polygamy was never to be tolerated.

I laughed at this, but soon stopped when another woman took up the lesson, seriously, as if I had not interrupted. "Never rest till every matter is settled in the hut," she said. "Run like a house on fire from fighting in the house. Never, never argue inside. This brings bad luck forever."

"When children come," another woman was saying out of her turn, a very short, fat woman. She was only a few years older than me, and I thought she's playing at being wise. This made me giggle out loud and Bithathe had to pinch me in my side to shut me up.

"Name the boy after yourself," the plump young-wise one said above hanging breasts. "Boys take the mother's name. Girls take their father's name, so there can be balance between boy and girl," she looked, and sounded, like an adult ahead of her time, folding her arms across the second baby in her stomach.

"And never, never hit children," the grand old lady continued, "when children are naughty, tell them stories of our ancestors. Let them fear and listen." This the other women repeated many times. "They will fear and listen," "They will listen. No beating."—because abuse of children was, almost above all else, a very serious crime. It carried some of the worst penalties.

I was told that a husband could not sell a sheep or a cow belonging to his wife without her permission. A husband could not do anything, even with his own belongings, or carry on any business, without his wife's counsel.

I was instructed on the rules of etiquette—that I could punish my brothers if they disobeyed, for I was ruler of the hut when my elder sister was not there.

But I had stopped listening. I wanted to get back to the *kraal*, to see my girlfriends, to boast to them about my new wisdom. But the women had to complete their instruction:

Never break wind, never belch in front of other people, especially guests. "Spit on the ground, not in a little skin," I was warned. Not like the missionaries, who need pieces of white cloth to spit in, when the whole earth was there for them.

At last, I was allowed to go into the water, to cleanse myself. I ran joyfully into the river, for during my seven days of seclusion I could make no contact with water.

Makhulu followed me slowly, while the other women stood on the riverbank.

I sat down in the water, and the earth paused in soft blue waves of heat, joined by a smiling middle of the day sun. Together the sun and earth made miracles for me. A lone sardine swam past my feet in the shallow water. It had wandered away from its thousands of brothers and sisters through rough seas from Port Elizabeth[61] bay, thirty miles away. The little sardine had swum all that way to come and bless me on my special day!

Makhulu took her stick and struck the water three times. Then she sprinkled water all over my body and I gave a squeal as the cold water hit my hot body, hoping that Solkar could hear me.

Bithathe came to me. Gently she pulled me up and turned me around. She hung my first loincloth in front of me like a little apron, tying the string behind my back. A square piece of sheepskin, it hung over my private parts.

"That must never be taken down," Makhulu said softly so only I could hear her. "Never show your private parts to anybody now that you are a woman, only to your husband one day…" she said dreamily, as she wrapped my first adult *kaross* around me. The sheepskin cloak was placed with the woolly side against my body, wrapping me in the softness of love.

At last, I was a real woman.

One of the women came up to me and gave me a bag made from the skin of a lizard, with tassels hanging down each end. Bithathe put this around my neck. "You can keep your trifles and trinkets in this," she giggled through a bright smile.

O how wonderful! By the time we danced our way back to the *kraal*—with me leading all the other women—I had over my ankles several layers of dried sheep-gut twisted into circular shapes, a necklace and bracelet of coral and freshly polished copper bracelets.

"The bracelets come from all our mothers," Bithathe said, for they were passed down from woman to woman in the family, from ancient times to me, as each of us celebrated our *!Habab*. "They come from one great-grandfather," Bithathe told me. "He gave a Dutch man a cow for it thousands of moons ago."

The women danced behind me as we ran along, their naked, bare breasts (unlike mine which were firm), swinging in time to their stamping feet. The singing and clapping of our happiness echoed into the hills.

As we came near to the *kraal* the children, who had been waiting along the way, came running behind us.

But the men stayed well hidden, for they could join the group only when the women had feasted.

And what a feast it was!

The day before, Tata had killed a sheep and drained its blood (the same blood which, mixed with herbs into a thick paste, Makhulu had rubbed over my body before sending me to the river that morning). The cooked sheep was ready and Makhulu was the first to eat from it.

Then all the healthy women ate and drank beer, made from stamped, boiled roots mixed with honey. A potent, bubbling mixture, it had stood covered for days and it made me light-headed and very, very happy.

The women stayed up all night with me dancing, gossiping, telling me secrets which made my cheeks burn.

Just before the sun rose the next morning, when the embers were low, Makhulu lit a long pipe. She passed it around to all of us. I could not believe that I was now a woman, allowed to smoke with the other women, for the children had long ago gone to sleep.

The pipe was our final treat before the party started again with the arrival of the new day and the men. It was filled with a sweet-smelling tobacco, which Tata had bought from the Dutch. The tobacco made me cough. But something was doing nice things inside my head.

Years later, in a faraway land, I found out that the *dagga* which was mixed in with the tobacco, is called marijuana by the English.

Rain

The Rain Ceremony is buried deep in my heart. When later my life became hard, many times, my mind would hold the Rain Ceremony up in front of sadness as a mirror of hope.

Tata was doing the preparations. The whole day he had been very busy, checking that everyone had done their tasks. He ran about, shouting orders, his thin bandy legs wobbling from side to side. They stuck out from under his goat-skin loincloth like two bent bows.

He had hardly any hair on his face or on his head, so I can never understand why the Dutch people gave him the family name *Baartman*. That means man with beard, and my father hardly had any hair! Sometimes I think that they gave it as a joke, as they did with other people. Some of my friends have the family name Elephant when they are small, with small feet and small ears and light-coloured skins. They do not look like any elephant I have seen. One friend is named Happiness. I wish I was given that name. Never mind, there are many people in my homeland called Baartman, so it can't be such a bad family name to have.

Anyway, as the sun set *Meneer Baartman* walk*ed* out of the *kraal*. He went out to have a smoke. I knew that he needed to be alone. I watched as he frowned, sitting there, thinking.

His brown face was creased. He looked up at the sky, which was clear and still.

I was standing on one of the *koppies*[62] looking down onto our *kraal* at the rounded shapes of the huts, a circle of upside-down baskets against a blue sky. Not a rain cloud was in sight.

I watched as Tata carefully made a pipe. He lit it. Then he sat smoking quietly, the hollow bone pipe clicking wetly against his teeth, which were stained brown with tobacco. He bit down on his pipe as he concentrated.

When he was finished, he lifted himself off the ground. I could see how tired he was, for he was hardly able to get his small frame off the ground. I loved my Tata so very much. I felt I had to be there to protect him, in case something happened to him, for our mama was dead and I knew he missed her. He walked tiredly back to the *kraal* and I followed him.

I followed him as he walked in through the side gate through which they would, not many days later, be carrying his body. Thanks to our ancestors, we did not yet know this.

A cow had wandered into the centre of the *kraal*. Tata ran through, past the girls' huts, and chased it away. The cow just wanted to lie down, when she changed her mind and flopped about comically before she could stand up, and run ahead of Tata, who was right behind her. As she mooed, I laughed, and I had a feeling that I had seen that happen before. I tried to remember, but could not, and carried on watching Tata's movements.

He lit the fire with the wood which the young boys had carried in earlier that day as people started to come into the centre of our *kraal*. I went to stand with my middle sister on the outer edge of the crowd. We were standing near the boys' hut. We went to stand there because we wanted to be there when the boys came out to do their dance.

I leaned against the young sapling branches which made up the frame of the hut. I pushed my nose into the reed mat wall and the deep smell left its wholeness like footprints deep inside my mind.

I was wearing the necklace which Solkar had given me. My happiness was complete.

Solkar had given me the necklace early that morning, when my sister, Lindiwe, and I went to fetch the water for the day from the dam. We were just stepping out of the gate and were walking down the dust path when Solkar came over the hill.

He was walking before the rising sun and his shadow walked ahead of him and greeted us quietly. He was wearing his big smile and I looked down shyly. Solkar was able to make my heart race in excitement as nobody else had ever done, just by being near me. My dear sister, Lindiwe, greeted him and just kept on walking, like a wise friend would.

"I have something special for you, small one," Solkar said. I was standing in front of this very handsome, important man, feeling just the way he was describing me. I smiled up at him and winked against the sun, which peeped past his large frame.

Solkar stepped up to me, real close, and whispered, "I have spoken with your Tata. He has given permission for us to become betrothed!"

My eyes opened, shut and opened again. I could not believe that this was happening to me!

"Will you marry me, please Thandi?"

At that age, I did not know that another, wiser, woman might have waited a bit, waited to be asked again, not wanting to seem too eager.

"Yes, yes, yes!" I laughed, with my hand over my mouth. I did not want Lindiwe to hear how very excited I was.

Solkar reached into the smart ostrich-skin pouch which hung down by his side. He brought out the most beautiful necklace I had ever seen.

He drew me closer, put the string around my neck and tied it behind, while kissing me gently on the cheek.

"Thank you, my small one. Soon you will be my wife." He kissed me on the mouth and my knees almost caved in.

"Thandi, where are you?" I heard Lindiwe call. Of course, life had to go on. I ran to meet my sister, holding the tortoise shell in my hand, pressing it against my breast. The trees around us whispered a blessing and looked blue-green and soft, and my sister's face lit up. She looked at me with an open smile of love and happiness as she held up the lovely shell which seemed to reflect the blueness and greenness of the trees back to them.

The necklace Solkar gave to me never left my neck from that day on.

That evening, the evening of the Rain Dance, was warm and humid, after a day which is forever covered in waves of merriment in my heart. The heat from the fire made the air stand still. Tata was busy preparing for the Dance. He moved around, now in the circle of the *kraal* shouting orders, then going through the cow gate to stand in the shadows.

Eventually he stood very still, next to the girls' hut, waiting for the men to arrive. When they came, he led the procession back into the centre of the *kraal*, ahead of them.

My breath became one with the silence which crept into the *kraal* as the men entered. Even the animals were quiet.

The men shuffled past us, carrying the cow which they had just killed. The cow hung with her feet pointing up to the dark skies in prayer. The calf inside her large belly lay still. It, too, was dead. Only pregnant cows were chosen to be sacrificed. They were given to Nature Mother as a plea, so that we could receive much water and food.

All the people were quiet, waiting. Tata showed the men how to carefully lower the pregnant cow onto the ground next to the fire. Then he slowly cut the cow's ribcage open. When it was open, the other men stepped forward and helped him.

They cut out a rib from each side of the cow's body. Then the men skinned the cow. They worked quickly. At the same time, some of the men cut out the fat from under the skin and dropped it into a pile near the fire.

I had seen this only once before, when I was very little, so seeing it again was very new to me. Tata cut out chunks of the meat and handed it to two men who were standing next to him. They passed the meat around, a chunk for each of the older men, who had gone to sit in an inner circle around the fire.

Next the boys came out of their hut. They lined up and waited quietly.

The old men stood up one by one, took a piece of fat from the pile and threw it into the fire. Clouds of thick smoke spiralled and disappeared up into the sky, promising safe journeys into the next life to all of us.

All went quiet. No one moved.

Tsui/Goab, the Creator, had arrived. Tsui/Goab, the Great He, Creator of all that lives, Maker and Sender of Rain, had turned his face to His people. All the people stood in silence.

Then the old men put the meat into the fire to roast.

And the young men started to dance.

It was a special dance, the Rain Dance. It could take place only upon the rise of the New Moon, which now hung clearly in the sky, far away.

The young men closed their eyes and murmured under their breath as they danced in a large circle around the older men. The words were inside their mouths. Kholisi, my elder brother, was leading the young men. He murmured with them, for he knew what they were saying. Each one was praying that the Mantis would settle on him, pleading that he might be the Chosen One.

"May I be the One! May I be the Chosen One through whom growth and prosperity will come to my people!" the boys broke out in song together, faces raised to the skies.

"…Growth and prosperity will come to my people!" all the women echoed in the high, clear notes of the young, joined by deep, croaky sounds forced through tobacco-coated older throats.

Then the old men removed the cooked meat from the fire and handed it out. The coals were dying down.

Each man pulled out a few strands of his hair and placed it on the burning coals. The old men rose into the smell of burning hair. Then they closed their circle tightly around the fire. The old men bent their knees and urinated over the burning coals.

Then they moved back slowly, with respect, heads bowed, as they faced the setting sun. Tsui/Goab, His Body in the smouldering coals and His Spirit in the smoke of hair and urine rising up, waited quietly, and we felt His presence.

The young men then moved forward and copied their elders.

Tata was the first to reach for his flute-reed. He held it to his chest and started moving around the fire. Then the other men, each with a hollow reed in his hand, moved with him. At first slowly, then faster, they opened up the circle, moving further and further back, away from the fire, and the boys followed them.

I waited with the other women, eager for our turn to come.

Raising their flutes to their lips, the men and boys played the mournful melodies which stayed with me for the rest of my life. In perfect harmony, they played as they danced. I watched my two brothers, one a man and one a boy, and my heart was filled with pride. The music passed in thrills down each muscle of my body.

Then we women stood up in a big circle outside the men. We raised our arms, waiting. Our bodies, our minds and thoughts were one with each other and I felt proud to be part of it all. I waited with them for the rhythm of the men's stamping feet to synchronise with the beat of my heart.

Then we started dancing.

We moved in the opposite direction to the men. We clapped our hands in perfect timing to their flutes, to their voices and to their feet.

Then we women started to hum. At first, it was only a whisper, in time to the gentle swish of the breeze through the leaves. Then the sound swelled and became low and long. We mimicked the river as it cried out for water.

"New Moon," we started to sing, our voices rising in urgency. "Please protect our families. Protect us as the Old Moon protected us throughout the long drought!" we pleaded.

I became intoxicated with the dance. We had to take small, graceful steps. We had to sway in time to the music. We had to push out from our hips, lifting our hands at the same time, clapping. We had to concentrate.

"Dear Moon, Mother Moon, New Moon," we pleaded.

And as we passed a hollowed tree trunk which stood between the huts, we scooped up honey beer into our thirsting throats.

We did not stop dancing. Around, around we went. Faster and faster, in circles which opened and closed, opened and closed in time to our laments and pleas to Tsui/Goab to bless us with Rain. The flutes became louder and louder and we sang higher and higher in ecstasy and expectancy.

Then we all stopped together. All our feet came to a complete standstill at the same time, as if the Great Conductor Tsui/Goab had held up his hand, saying "Enough!"

We paused with our arms stretched out far above our heads. Then we gave a single loud clap which cut into the sky.

"Tsui/Goab!" we cried together. My face was covered in sweat and so was everyone else's.

We turned our faces to the New Moon and then, together, we all bowed our heads. We paused together.

So we continued, dancing, pleading, receiving, until flesh and spirit became one.

We carried on until we could go no further, until one by one we sank to the ground, to lie where we had fallen, in exhausted slumber.

The sun woke us up with gentle warmth early next morning as the cattle walked with nosey curiosity into the centre of the *kraal,* to see why they had not been put out to graze.

As we stirred, we knew that the Maker of Rain had accepted our sacrifice.

Tata Is Dead[63]

My childhood was filled with gunfire. The Dutch took our land and stole our pastures. They fought the people from Britain, who asked us to help them. Our people were glad to help because we thought that the British would give us back our land.

They called them *Bushmen* wars. They captured our women, slaughtered our men. They took our children. They took our women's breasts, dried them, and used them to carry their tobacco in.

Eventually, I did not know who was fighting whom.

All I know is that my father, Tata, gave his life to bring peace, which never came. We, Khoekhoen (Khoikhoi) joined with the San and the Xhosa to fight against the horrible Dutch. Then the British turned on us, and would not give us our land back. Then the Dutch ganged up with the British against us.

These things my older brother, Kholisi, spoke about. "They are forcing us against each other," I heard him say when he was sitting with his friends around the fire. "They forced us to join their armies. Now they steal our farms."

And this is how Tata was murdered.

Tata used to go to the Cape to take cattle, to sell them there. One day he never came home. A *Bosjeman*[64] of the San tribe killed him.

We were preparing the celebrations for my wedding to Solkar. Each new day arrived with its open arms of excitement as it called me to be the future wife of the son of the *kaptein*.

But the rain would still not come. The wind kept chasing the clouds away and the sun turned the veld dry that year. The dryness was lasting for a long time. The trees which had been young when I became a woman were growing fast, even faster than my body. I had been a woman for many moons by then.

The drought was at its worst that winter. The cold weather had set in early, very early. The animals were cold and thirsty. No rain would pass over the Gamtoos river, and he became as thin as the animals he was supposed to keep alive. The north-westerly winds promised rain, but as the clouds approached the lowlands, they would be driven back by the winds which sweep across the inlands, down to the sea. We would watch the clouds with disappointment, through eyes pressed together into small slits, hands cupped over them, as all peoples who live their lives in the sun have to do.

The animals became more and more listless as the days grew shorter. And the people despaired.

Yet nothing could touch my happiness.

That is why I felt that what happened was in a way my fault. While the animals starved, I lived my life to the full. I was going to get married and nothing, nothing could dampen my happiness.

In some ways, I blamed myself for bringing bad luck to my people. I saw the animals. I did, in passing, notice their sad eyes, sunken cheeks and aching ribcages. I knew that they were dying because the rain would not come, but in my happiness I could not feel their pain.

Disrespect for our animals, I know, brings bad luck. Why had I ignored their suffering and done nothing? I knew the cattle were losing their young at birth. It was much talked about. And when the old men and the old women ate the prematurely born foetuses, I and my young friends were relieved, for we were spared the unpleasant-smelling food.

When the old, ailing cows were slaughtered as was the custom, and fed to the dogs, I and my young friends teased the dogs and chased after them as they dragged the bones through the dry, dusty earth in front of the other hungry animals.

I was yet half an adult woman, half a child.

If only my friends and I had not made the heavens so angry that night.

The grownups stared into the sky with fear and hope and talked about nothing but the rain which would not come. The guns of the white armies were echoing over the hills as we sat around our fires. For I was a woman now and had joined them there.

"I can steal that young goat," I boasted to my friends, still acting like the child which I wanted to be. The goat was tied up and was to be killed to feed the dogs.

I stole the goat. Then I let it loose and we chased the dogs after it. I felt great, as the other girls followed me.

But I felt that the one who caused a curse to stay behind when I let the goat loose. I had brought the anger of the sun upon my people.

The next morning I had a heavy feeling in my heart. I felt a great fear in me, a bad taste in my mouth. I did not want Tata to leave the *kraal*. I knew that I was not supposed to go hunting any longer. I could not ask to go with Tata, but I needed to be with him. So, when he walked through the gate into the fields, I followed him. As soon as the men had disappeared over the hill, I followed them. I felt in my heart that I had to make sure that Tata was safe.

Only later could I admit to myself that I knew all along that Tata would not come back. I should have warned Tata. I should have spoken with Solkar because he, too, went with the men.

As I was trailing behind them, the men suddenly ran over a clearing, heading for some trees, their *kieries*[65] held high above their heads. I had to wait for them to run in amongst the trees before I could follow them. I rushed over the open field, when I noticed that Tata was well behind the other men, who were all much younger. I waited, for I did not want to be seen.

If only I had not waited, I would have seen what happened next.

While the other men were swallowed up in the semi-darkness of the forest, and before I could reach the first tree for cover, a *Bosjeman* jumped from behind a tree and drove a spear into Tata's chest.

I heard his gurgle above the crunching of fleeing feet on dead leaves.

I ran to Tata. I was now no longer worried that I could be seen. I dropped down next to him and cradled his head in my arms. His eyes opened, fixed, glazed.

"Tata," I cried. Slowly his eyes moved towards my face. They opened wider in recognition. Then his head fell against my chest and blood gushed across my arms.

I would never know for how long I sat there, frozen in shock, nor how I got back to the *kraal.*

"Tata…Tata is…," I gasped, as I pulled my elder brother Kholisi by his arm. Not knowing what it meant, yet recognising the urgency, Kholisi jumped up and ran after me as I sped straight back across the veld.

But we were too late. Tata was dead.

And Solkar never came back either.

During the weeks which followed every detail of what had happened was stamped on my soul forever.

It was never known why Tata had been killed. People made up different stories.

"The *Bosjemans*[66] were jealous of Tata's white ox and killed him for it," an old man said. This might have been true, because Tata's white ox, a sign of our family's prosperity, had disappeared since his death.

"Tata ate from the flesh of a hare," another said.

"He took honey from a bees' nest belonging to the *Bosjemans*," a woman whispered.

The elders spoke when they thought I was not listening, for they would go silent when younger people were about.

Those stories upset me more. I did not know what to believe. They saddened me. I was unhappy, confused. Should I cry for my Tata, or should I mourn for Solkar? Where was Solkar? I knew that I would never see him again and my world had truly collapsed.

I was sad, yet I could not cry. I shed no tears then or later, though why, I would never understand. Perhaps my grief was too deep for tears. This is how I felt as the time passed.

In any event, crying for the dead was the privilege of the older women. They wailed and got all the attention. The younger ones were forgotten.

The older women, with their high-pitched cries of grief, enjoyed the tongue-clicking sympathy of the sombre men, who bent over their pipes in quiet support.

I suffered in obedient, resentful silence.

Pieter Cezars

We could not sleep the night before Tata's burial. We four sisters sat in Bithathe's hut all night long. We sat around the open fire, not talking with each other, awake and sad, while Bithathe's two young children turned restlessly in their sleep behind us on the earthen floor.

The night was long and soulful. It was eerily quiet. The last three nights had been a commotion of wailing, which had woken up the animals of the wild. The women's cries mixed with deep throated growls and the hyena's mocking laughter far between the hills. Even the mountains were crying as they echoed the cries back across the veld.

Next morning the older men took Tata's body out of his hut and the older women bent Tata's body double—like a baby inside a thin woman's belly.[67] They put him into his favourite *kaross*, sewing the skins together carefully.

And put him into the cold earth.

The men carried Tata through the poster gate, walking slowly, his head facing the rising sun. My heart stood still in coils of cold steel.

The big hole was ready, waiting. They sat Tata up, on his backside, still bent over like a baby to be born, they put him into the hole. Then they filled it, first with small stones, then with earth, and lastly with big stones.

Then Kholisi, my elder brother, burnt Tata's hut, as he had to do. All Tata's clothing, his hunting purse, pipes, eating utensils and *karosses*, everything, was taken into the hut and burnt with it. The flames went up with the last communal moan as the people expressed their final grief.

The last embers died down and the sun set behind the huts.

Then all hell broke loose.

The nightmare which followed is all in pieces in my head. I cannot remember everything that happened.

Gunfire lit up the sky above the dying fires and people scattered all over. We screamed, ran, grabbed children as we fled, where to, we did not know. We had to get away from the guns, that was all we knew. As some of us, men as well as women and children, fell and died, we stumbled over each other, with no time to help the dying.

All our men, our fathers, our brothers, our lovers were shot and killed.

And some of the women, unfortunate women, were bound and taken away by the evildoers, far from our beloved forests and driven away with a thousand insults. One of the women was one sister of mine. I never saw her again.

My people fought. My people lost.

But inside me, painted on my soul, imprints of a fighter could not be removed.

Somehow my second sister, Lindiwe, Bithathe, her two children and I, survived. We ran into the hills, I carried Bithathe's youngest child who had not yet seen two summers, and my sister pulled the older child along with her. We ran into the hills with a few other women.

We knew the way through the forest, which the white people did not know. We ran until our breath was burning so much it melted our throats and sent spears into our heads.

We stopped only when the sound of the guns faded across the hills and we could sit close with our arms around each other, in silence.

Sara, Pieter's wife was with us. We knew Pieter and Sara. They had a piece of land not far from where our *kraal* was.

Pieter used to be a slave, then the missionaries bought his freedom. Pieter used to work at the church with them, and he could read and he could write and we respected him very much.

"Sara, Sara!" we heard a far cry, after a long time, when we were sitting in silence, too scared to speak to each other in case the animals gave us away to the Dutch.

"Sara, where are you? Sara!"

"It's Pieter," Sara was excited. She stood up and shouted (although she thought she was whispering because she had her hand cupped over her mouth as if she was speaking softly).

"Pieter! Pieter!" she called. She was so excited that she stumbled across Bithathe who swore out loud, which was the first time I ever heard my sister using ugly language.

Sara ran, stumbled across a tree in the dark and stood still, because she could not see into the dark. She had woken the animals up and we heard squeaks and rushing feet scrambling into the forest floor around us.

Then Pieter appeared and we felt safer. Our younger brother, Bhundi, followed behind him. It took a while for us to realise that all the other men had been killed. It took the whole night for us to realise that we were all alone, that our older brother had been killed as well and that we had to depend on Pieter to help us.

As the morning came close, and after Pieter and Sara had sat alone away from us, talking softly, Pieter came across to us. Bithathe was half asleep, lying between the two children. I was sitting staring through the trees as the smile of the sun, as always, made the skies change from sombre darkness into pink sympathy and understanding.

"Bithathe," Pieter said quietly, his voice deep and strong. Bithathe sat up slowly, pulling herself away from little arms and legs.

"I would like to take you and Thandi and the children to the Cape of Good Hope. Your husband," he said, looking straight at Bithathe, "Xolokwa, is safe. He will be arriving soon. I saw him run this way and called to him. Bhuti can come too. We would like that."

Bithathe looked at me and I nodded solemnly.

"Yes, we would like that too," she said, looking down with disbelief, for neither of us could see how we could ever get to the Cape, which lay across many mountains and rivers. Our hearts were too raw and our minds were too sore to understand what Pieter was saying.

But Pieter had a plan. "I have started a small farm in Cape Town," he said. "I need help. I do not have money, but I hope that I can make it good for you."

We looked up at the black man with his kind smile and his open heart and knew that we were, after all, safe.

At that time, the British had been at the Cape of Good Hope for many years. Pieter told us that he wanted to leave anyway, because of all the fighting. He had planned this for a long time.

"We are all together now," he said. "I am a free man and I can take you on as my servants at the Cape." This we felt happy about, for it was good to be with one of our own.

At another time, under different circumstances, I would have been very happy to see the big town at last.

I accepted Pieter's plan with much sadness.

Then Xolokwa, Bithathe's husband, appeared through the trees. My beloved sister Bithathe stood up and cried. It was the first, and last time, I saw my brave sister cry.

Cape Town

The rain came thirty days later.

By that time we had travelled far south. The journey had taken longer than it would have, for we went along the flat, level paths around the coast rather than going inland, over mountains. When we got to small hills, Pieter went around them, not over them, because he did not want the children to get too tired.

We enjoyed the nights, when we would camp out on the beach and swim in the warm waters of the seas. And we would catch sea food, and make a fire, and eat under wide, open skies with winking stars for night lights.

When we came to the big rivers, Pieter would take his horse through the water and we would get out of the wagon and push it through the water, swimming next to the wagon, which carried the children.

Sometimes, when the water was very deep, Pieter would find a big log from a willow tree, for its wood is light and floats easily on water. He would take all day to chop out its inside so we could sit in the little *amass* to cross the deep rivers. On those days we were very afraid, for we would lie looking up at the sky on our little tree boat and the river would be angry and try to shake us out.

By the time the rain came, we could actually see the big Table Mountain. We could not move any further and we had to camp out near a river, for the rain came down suddenly, very hard. The rain was angry. It rode on a wind, which wanted to drive us back from where we came. We sat huddled under trees for hours, waiting for nature's anger to subside.

At last the rain stopped, and with a burst, the sun came through into a pale blue sky. And a rainbow came to show us that all was well. It hung in front of the big mountain in the distance and showed us that we were going to be happy in Cape Town.

For us, Cape Town turned out the right place to be. It had a thousand houses, which stood in straight, clean, lines. It had canals which led from the river along the streets.

We were given two huts on the little farmland, which Pieter owned. My two sisters, Lindiwe and Bithathe, and the children, worked in the fields for Pieter, picking grapes, for he was making wine, which he sold to the British. I worked in their little house, in Riebeekstraat,[68] in the centre of Cape Town. They had no children. I cleaned and cooked for them, and learned about the ways of the people of the big city.

My middle sister, Lindiwe, and I loved to go and stand in the square. There were four squares and one market, which we loved to go to when we were not working. We would watch the soldiers exercising on the parade grounds near the seashore, next to the castle where they lived in their barracks.

It was Pieter who first called me Saartjie. He said it playfully.

"Saartjie," he said, looking at me, his brown eyes lighting up.

"Small Sara?" his wife said, amused, because her Dutch name was Sara. Big Sara. Everyone laughed, because we did look alike. Our bodies had small waists, short tops, with large hips and big behinds. I soon started wearing Sara's clothes although the skirts were a bit long for me.

Lindiwe and I would stand for hours gazing at the Cape Town gentry with their carriages pulled by horses. These were different from the ox-wagons of the settler farmers. The gentlewomen wore strange dresses which joined bodice and skirt into one long drape. It looked as if the women were choking under their tight-fitting necklines, with frills on top of high stand-up collars.

The foreign men looked most ridiculous of all, with their clean-shaven, painted faces, wigs and pantaloons. We nudged each other and giggled at them.

"The little boys look just like girls," Lindiwe said to Bithathe, who laughed, for the boys dressed just like the girls, who looked just like their mothers.

The crowds, men and women, slaves and freemen. All amazing.

Soon we made friends with other young servants, mostly slave girls. Once we found out where the Hottentot Regiment soldiers were living, we did not stay away from the young soldiers for long.

Me and my sister and our friends became an important part of the regiment. The soldiers made us feel important. On Sunday afternoons, when we went walking along the white beaches of Cape Town, the young men would show off how much they knew of the history of Africa's most southern city.

The waters off the tip of Africa rushed from opposite directions, each fighting to keep the territory to themselves, pushing and colliding to get each other out of the way.

In the same way, the different nations had tried to claim Cape Town for themselves. Besides the British, the Dutch and before them the French and long, long ago, the Portuguese, and there were slaves from far lands as well.

They spoke different languages. People who looked like us, but also looking different, some yellow, some white, some black. Some with straight noses, some with flat noses, others with tiny noses and different hair. Some of them spoke with open mouths, making sounds like cats meowing. They had strange names and came from countries with stranger names like Indonesia, Malaysia, China and India. They came with funny habits to our land, wearing weird and wonderful clothes, and eating food with wild smells.

But yet they were like us, for many of our children, like some of theirs, had flat, slanted eyes and small noses with white fathers who had bought their women and children out of slavery.

But the Khoikhoen had been there before time had a memory, before the arrival of all those peoples. Our ancestors had sometimes fought against, but more often welcomed, the settlers from the north, black and white. But we were there first, we were born there before everyone else. We were the first people of the Earth. We were the First Nation and our Cape Town belonged to us.

I soon grew to love my Cape Town.

Paddy

Things were happening very fast that year. There was a fight between the white people. The people from Britain landed at Blaaubergstrand. The people from Holland, who were in charge of the Cape, were chased away.

This was what changed my luck, because with the soldiers from Britain came Paddy. He was a drummer in the British Army.

I went to collect the household water late that day. I don't know why I did this, but if I had not done so, I would never have met him. It was a long walk down the Heerengracht to the water fountains. I went to the fountain in Caledon Square and not the one which is closer to my work. I had to walk a bit further, but I liked doing that because it took me around the parade grounds where I met my girlfriends.

I was with one of my friends and we were walking and talking. I was carrying the empty water bucket in one hand. The other hand was under the white apron which I wore over my blouse and skirt. I was wearing one of my oxhide *karosses* to keep warm. Then my friend pushed me, and I tried to get my hand out from under the apron, but was not quick enough, so I fell forward and tripped. The bucket went flying.

I fell straight into the arms of a soldier who was walking towards us with his friend.

"Careful now, lassie," he said in a voice full of laughter. I felt awkward, because everyone was looking at me.

"Paddy's the name," he said, his hand still around my waist. "And what might your name be?" he asked, his eyes on me, as if we were alone.

I was tongue-tied. I knew so few words of English and I was afraid that if I answered him, he might ask further questions and then I might not be able to answer in his language. I felt hot and embarrassed.

I was sure that he knew this. He laughed naughtily at me, his nose puckering up. Then he let me go.

"Saartjie," my friend said because I did not know what to say.

"Sar-key," he said, and for the first time the name given to me by Pieter, inherited from the Dutch people, sounded like music. "And what might that name mean?" He was looking straight at me. I did not know what to say. "And what might your Khoi name be, then?" he asked, smiling.

"Thandi," I said in a croak. Paddy bowed and I laughed. My friend squealed with laughter. Paddy looked really funny.

"Can you speak English, Sar-key?" he whispered while the others were laughing. I nodded. Then, confused, I shook my head.

"Then I will teach you. Do you want me to teach you to speak English, Sar-key?"

I nodded again but I was very embarrassed so I grabbed my bucket and walked away as fast I could, my heart pounding.

I saw Paddy again a few days later. I was standing on the parade alone one evening, watching two Khoi men playing around on the ground. The men were sitting opposite each other, shouting at each other as if they were arguing. I had stopped off in the marketplace behind the government buildings where the government's slaves lived.

"Sar-key," I heard his soft voice behind me. Blood rushed to my cheeks. I did not turn around. I pretended that I had not heard him and kept my eyes on the two men on the ground.

"Sar-key," he said again. This time I could feel his body heat. He had come closer and was standing with his body lightly touching me from behind. He had spoken close to my ear, and put his arms around me from behind. Then he moved to stand next to me, keeping his arm around my waist.

I was hot with embarrassment. I looked around to make sure nobody I knew was there. He did not move his arm away from me. The feelings which ran through me came out in a giggle, and I had to turn my face away to hide my smile.

The men were throwing their bodies from side to side, tossing their arms in all directions. They laughed loudly and threw their arms up into the air in turn. One of them jumped up and down, followed by the other. They came to face each other, sitting on their haunches, now moving a fist around on the ground between them.

"What are they doing, Sar-key?" Paddy had also turned to watch them. He spoke without turning his head away from them.

This gave me a quick chance to see him from the side. He was not very tall, for my eyes were level with his shoulder. His brown hair was much darker than his beard, which was a reddish colour. His mouth was always smiling, under a moustache. He had laughter lines running from his eyes across his temples.

He turned to face me and then, for the first time, I saw his hazel eyes. I dropped my eyes. I was feeling awkward.

I wanted to tell him that the two men were playing a game, where one man had to hide a small stick in one of his hands, and the other one had to find it. I wanted to tell him this and much more, but the words would not come.

That day was the first time we were alone together. It took me a long time to start putting sentences together in Paddy's language. He did all the talking.

After that day, I took many walks with him. On Sunday afternoons, we would meet up and go to the jetty at Table Bay and meet his friends. Or we would walk to the Rogge Bay Battery, where he showed off. He jumped on the platform next to the guns and pretended to be hanging from the cannon. I loved being with him.

We would go walking in the Avenue which runs through Cape Town Gardens. Once, sitting under a huge old tree near some bushes, a sunbird hopped past us. Paddy put his finger to his lips and we sat still, waiting to see what the bird would do. Everything was good because Paddy was next to me. The bird walked past us, jumped onto a bright orange aloe and pushed its beak deep into the food pipe of the flower. When the bird withdrew its beak it looked straight at us, a large golden question mark of pollen between its eyes. It winked at me and flew away and life was glorious.

Everything was perfect, everybody and everything was part of my joy. Even the ducks swam a dance with their necks moving in time to the music in my heart.

"Kyk," I said to Paddy, pointing to a shy *duiker*[69] which had stopped to stare at us. Then I stifled a laugh, for I remembered that I had spoken to Paddy in Dutch and that he could not understand what I had said.

"Look," I quickly translated. It was too late, for the little antelope had already disappeared into the bushes on its wobbly hind legs. Paddy laughed at the way I mixed my tongues, and I was not sure whether to laugh with him or how to show my joy.

But Paddy could also be serious. He told me many things. Things like his childhood memories, in his country called Ireland. It was very far way, so far away that the distance could not be measured by mountains and hills. He stopped when I could not understand, and he would search for words which would be familiar to me.

He told me about how the English had done the same bad things to his people as they, and the Dutch before them, had done to mine. I wanted to tell him about how they had killed my people, but I could not, because I did not know enough of his language.

I loved the way he spoke. He told me how the English chiefs had sent their people to settle on land which belonged to his people, how they were driven off their farms. I wanted to say how sorry I felt for him, because I knew the feelings, although I did not understand all the words.

"My father was very poor," Paddy explained slowly, so that I could understand. And when the snow fell from one new moon to the next, he said, then the potatoes, which looked like the *gabes* which grew on the Cape Town hills, rotted in the ground.

I could feel the cold when he told of how his little toes had grown large with water under an itchy, dry skin in animal-skin shoes which gaped and let in the frost and mud.

As we spent more time together, I lost my shyness. I loved life and I was eager to learn. I struggled to learn the new language. The strange words of his language were sticky. They clung to my tongue with the stubbornness of a baby monkey clinging to its mother's bosom, jumping off only with much coaxing and effort from Paddy, and gasps of exasperation from me.

When it rained, we would climb up the rocks at the foot of Devil's Peak mountain, and sit in an overhanging cave, near the blockhouses called King and Queen, catching glimpses of the blueness of Table Bay.

That winter is forever to remain painted in soft colours in my memory.

We stayed out late at night. We could do this, because we, Khoikhoen, were not part of the curfews which were meant for slaves.[70]

Paddy and I enjoyed our freedom.

Our favourite walk was along the canal bank, where the Dutchmen greeted Paddy with a *wel te rusten* as we passed. I felt very proud the day when I could tell Paddy that it meant rest well in his language.

Time passed in a haze of happiness which dreams are made of. We were young. We spent every moment we could together. And, as young folks would, we ignored the signs. When together, we were totally engrossed in each other.

We did not notice the disapproving frowns of social custom or the pursed lips of protocol.

Paddy Leaves

Disapproval came in the form of Hendrick Cezars.

Hendrick knew that the Irish soldier had been visiting me. By this time I was working for Hendrick and Anna Catharina, because she was expecting a child and needed help in the home. Pieter Cezars thought it was none of his business whom I saw. Hendrick made it his business.

I did not know that Paddy arrived at the house of Hendrick early one morning. He went straight to the back door because he expected me to open it. It was just his bad luck that Hendrick came to the door.

Anna Catharina told me this a long time later, when she saw me crying and I told her I could not understand why Paddy was not calling on me anymore.

She said she had heard him knock on the back door at least three times and Hendrick went to open it.

"Ja?" Hendrick barked. "What do you want!" he raised his voice, Anna Catharina said.

"I have a message for Sar-key, sir," Paddy said politely.

"She's not here." Anna Catharina said she was quite upset with Hendrick, because I was in the yard feeding the chickens.

"When will she be back, please, sir?"

"Dunno. What's the message?"

"Please tell her that I will be away for a few months. Will you please tell her that, sir, when she returns?"

"Ja." Hendrick closed the outer mosquito-mesh "in his face," Anna Catharina said.

Hendrick never gave the message to me.

Sangoma (Healer)

I waited for Paddy for a long time. I waited until I could no longer measure time. By this time, Anna Catharina was close to giving birth to her baby and I was there to look after her.

One evening I was sitting behind the house under a half moon. It felt like my life had turned itself upside down like an abandoned hut.

I was very worried.

I had a pain in my belly. Hot and hollow, then sharp and angry, it came and went. I closed my eyes and breathed deeply, and shadows of doubt in the form of trees hung behind my closed eyelids. A warm berg wind was sweeping across the ponds, into the trees behind me. They rustled. My arms came out in goose bumps.

My heart ached for Paddy, who had gone and forsaken me.

When the rising sun splashed, a creamy pink light from the east into the sky and woke the birds, I went back indoors.

I could not sleep. A nagging thought kept eating into my mind. I thought I knew what the pains in my stomach were about, but I would not admit it to myself. I could not be sure, anyway.

So I lay there, for a long time, and finally I fell asleep.

I had been let down. I felt betrayed. Paddy was not the man I had thought he was. He had left me and my body was aching and I felt ill. Like the secrets of the pain in my belly, something was amiss, something was not telling me what was wrong.

Next morning the pain attacked me real bad. Bithathe was there in the little back room with me. She saw me bending forward, trying to pick up her baby, then almost dropping the child as the pain gripped my stomach. Bithathe cried out and grabbed her baby from me.

"What's wrong, Thandi?" she demanded, concern on her face.

"I've got a pain here," I said. I rubbed the sides of my stomach.

"When did it start?"

I could not remember. I did not know. I pointed to the area above my tummy and ran outside to be sick.

Bithathe ran after me and told me to go back inside. She sent her eldest boy to go and call the healer.

I was afraid. Healers bleed people. They use sharp, double-bladed knives and long bits of iron with small knobs on their ends. They would place the knobs of iron over the fire and when glowing hot, they would press them into people's arms. The raw wound they covered with herbs mixed with freshly cooked, sweet milk. Or so I had heard.

I dreaded the arrival of the healer.

I had nothing to fear though. The healer who arrived was a woman. A wise old woman. She had many roots, dried animal gut, strings of herbs, bones and other bits of dried plant and animal around her neck. She looked just as dried out and wrinkled. But her creased, sun-burnt, brown face was kind.

She sat looking at me for a long while. She asked me about the pains, and I showed her where they were. They were on both sides of my stomach.

"Does it feel like a snake is in there?" was all she asked.

I was surprised the woman knew this. Yes, I nodded. That was exactly how the feeling had started the first time I had felt it. Almost a wriggling inside my belly, many times. As if a little snake was trying to move up and down, but not out.

I expected the healer to use her healing-stone to move a slimy animal out of my body. I sat with my eyes closed. I expected a *tokoloshe*[71] to come out of me, the wicked little green man who attacks children. I expected the *tokoloshe* to be pulled out through my navel, for it was living inside my warm body like a snake.

When I opened my eyes, I saw the old healer looking at me, a smile of wisdom on her lips. Her last tooth, a single bottom incisor, stained brown with years of tobacco chewing, pointed out and over her top lip.

The ligaments in her scrawny neck were taut and her bony body seemed almost to dangle from her neck, like a manikin on a string.

She did not ask any further questions. She did not want to know of any other movements, feelings or things. She did not touch me. But she knew.

"She is with child," she said to Bithathe with her single-toothed smile.

I was to stay indoors, she ordered. I was to remain still, else I would lose the baby, for my body was about to throw it out.

The news shocked Bithathe.

I went silent. I could not believe what the old lady had said. My silence infuriated Bithathe.

"Who? Who! Who did this to you?" she demanded over and over again.

I did not answer.

Destiny

But I knew when it was that it had happened.

It was the day when Paddy and I had walked to Zoutrivier, when he had asked me to go to his land with him.

"How would you like to go to Ireland?" he had said. Suddenly, unexpectedly, he had said this, while my warm toes were pushing into the cool, soft sand along the bank of the Liesbeeck River, and my mind was on the dark blueness of Table Mountain.

"Mmm." I was chewing a juicy *vygie*[72] which I had picked from the path next to the ponds where the figs grew wild.

"Ireland is very much like Cape Town, you know." He had reached for me, made me face him. Then he sat me down on a big boulder.

"There are beaches there, which look just like your beaches," he said. "One day, I'll take you to the southern coast of Ireland. There is a Bantry Bay there too, it looks just like the sea does from the other side of the mountain," he said, pointing to where the lone island, Robben Island, is.

I said nothing. He stopped often, hunting for Dutch words when he thought I could not understand what he was saying. I said nothing because I loved my country and did not want to leave my people. I loved to breathe in the beauty of my land.

It is my earth, which then was droning dozily around me as spring seeped intoxicating saps into her bloodstream and into mine.

But I loved to hear Paddy speak. I did not want to interrupt him. His pleasant voice wrestled with the strange, guttural words, when he tried to make me understand in a language which did not suit his tongue or mine.

"Saw Paddy. Sunday. Parade," I changed the subject.

"Were you there? Did you see me play the drums?" I nodded.

"I'll show you Khoikhoi drum," I offered. How I would love to hear him play one of my family drums, I thought, while I played to him on my *ramkie.*

We walked along in silence for a long while after that. I led the way, for I knew the path very well.

My mind was somewhere in the blue sky. I was walking slightly to the right and ahead of Paddy. He walked silently. We were enjoying the quiet heat of the day together, the butterflies hopping about at play.

I was feeling hot, so I unbuttoned the big blouse I was wearing and pulled it up and around my neck like a scarf. Next, to ease the tight string around my waist, I loosened the string slightly. I had my back to Paddy.

He came up behind me and put his arms around my neck. I liked that. He turned me around to face him and pulled me towards him. Together we sank onto the soft, white sand. The sun was blocked out by the outline of a head of curls as I closed my eyes, and Paddy came down onto me.

Time stopped.

And then I felt the most excruciating pain shoot through my belly. I pushed my head into his shoulder above me to stifle the cry which rose up. It took a few moments for Paddy to draw himself out of me.

"I'm sorry, Sar-key, really," he said, breathing heavily between my sobs. "I did not know it was the first time for you. Did it hurt you very much?"

He stroked my shoulder as he spoke, for I had turned my back to him so that I could double up against the pain. I lay on my side, both legs up against my chin, protecting my burning insides. I tried to move the little apron over my exposed lower body.

"Sar-key, talk to me, please," Paddy pleaded when I stopped crying. "I should have asked you first, I know. I'm sorry." I could not reply, although I was not angry with him. I was waiting for the pain to go away.

"Tell me you're not angry with me, Sar-key," he pleaded.

I felt sorry for him. I sat up slowly, painfully. I could not look into his eyes. I reached for the skirt, which was lying on the ground by my side, and swung it over my shoulders as I stood up. I walked slowly around a tree, out of his sight.

There I carefully wiped away the blood with the side of the skirt. Mixed with his life-food, the blood had turned into an attractive pink colour. The moment was intense. I went to sit down in a little stream and used the end of my skirt to wash myself down.

Paddy could not let me be. He walked towards me quietly, guilt all over his face. He sat down on a boulder next to me and pulled me up into his arms.

"Please don't be angry with me, Sar-key. I didn't know it was your first time. I'm so sorry."

I felt anything but anger. I felt shy and confused, but not angry. I felt inside me the stirrings of a wonderful, soft hunger, but not anger. My body felt soft as I leaned it against his strong body.

Then there was a next time. This time there was no guilt from either of us. He forgot his Catholic teachings. I forgot my instruction. The waves of our union ebbed and flowed in a sea of oblivion.

Many times, when I was standing on the little stage in the cold in England, and then in Paris, have I in my mind repainted the picture of that day, in brighter colours, with new paints, to keep my belief in Paddy firm.

****

I did eventually tell Bithathe Paddy's name.

Paddy. Paddy, the wayward Irishman, Bithathe kept saying in shock.

"To think that my sister, my little sister, had been coaxed into this, this shameful condition by the white man. Thandi, you who could have been married to a chief's son!"

Paddy had brought shame on our family. He would have to come and do his duty immediately.

She sent her husband to find Paddy.

But Paddy was not there. They thought he knew what had happened and had run away. He was avoiding his responsibilities.

They questioned me. Did I tell Paddy that I was with child? No, I did not. Perhaps he knows, anyway. He must know. He's a man. A man of the world who knows these things, Bithathe went on and on. She was very angry. She blamed the outsider. She thought I was innocent, had been tricked by the white man.

Paddy had to be found. He had to be forced into marriage.

Bithathe sent her husband to the soldier's quarters many times. He has gone inland, her husband came back to say. They did not know when he would return.

"Now he has run away!" Bithathe kept scolding me. "Now when your shame is growing big, he has run away."

Anna Catharina was not well. Her baby was due to arrive any day and I was kept very busy in the house. I would otherwise have had to go into complete isolation. I still did not leave the house—not even to fetch water—but this did not seem so bad, because I was kept busy in the house.

But I could not go out at all. I had to take my meals alone in the little room at the back of the small house. I was not allowed to be seen. The only time I was allowed to go out was when it was dark. Then I could only go into the yard.

I found it hard to accept my isolation. But it was nothing compared to the loneliness and rejection I felt inside.

Bithathe sometimes visited me at night, moaning and complaining about 'the white man', because she refused to say Paddy's name. I kept saying to her that he would come to me when he found out what was happening. She, on the other hand, could not believe that Paddy had not been told by any of his friends that I needed to see him.

Meantime Xolokwa, Bithathe's husband, did all he could to get hold of Paddy. He went to the barracks regularly, only to be told that Paddy was still away. Bithathe was convinced that Paddy had run away, back to his own country. She told me this, many times over.

Birth

The summer became hotter. My heart became heavier. I was feeling ill and drained, and the heat did not help.

Anna Catharina's baby was born, and this gave me things to do. I helped her with the baby and around the house because she was very frail, and Hendrick was a hopeless husband. He spent almost all his nights in the taverns in town. He had made friends with a doctor, I heard him tell Anna Catharina, and they were planning a business together.

The weather did not help. During the day the sun would scorch into my skin if I so much as went outside. I would rest inside in my little room and the walls would throw unbearable heat in. I would gasp in thirst and feel faint and listless most of the time.

At night the sun, from where it was watching from its perch in the darkness, would continue to be spiteful and suffocate me by heating up the air so I could not breathe properly. I would toss about on my little mat in the room, plagued by dreams and longing.

But still I hoped that Paddy would come.

The first pain bounced into my womb one night when I was sitting under the trees where nobody could see me, smoking a pipe. My pipe had gone out. I was about to light it again, when the pain jumped into me from nowhere, like a mischievous monkey, bouncing away immediately. I ran inside, in a panic. The next pain grabbed me as I sat down in my room.

I was worried. Anna Catharina was sleeping with the baby. I could not wake them up. I did not know if Hendrick was in the house, but I would not dare ask him to help me. So I stayed inside my room and lay down on my *kaross* on the floor.

Soon the pains came closer together. Tight metal clamps, they squeezed themselves around my body. They arched my back, then whipped me forward so that my head shook and blood flowed from my bottom lip which was clamped between tight jaws. The pain left me gasping.

I would sit completely still between the contractions, suspended, waiting, every nerve in my body taut.

Nobody had prepared me for the intensity of childbirth. Neither was there anybody there to help me.

So I took the pain. And then some more.

I chewed the insides of my cheeks between attacks, waiting to sit the next one through. I lay on my back and dug my nails into the bottom of my thighs as I pulled them up and into the pain. I fought nature until there were hardly any intervals between attacks.

Then reason and respect for tradition and custom deserted me. I had to go for help. I stood up. The pain grabbed me again. I threw myself against the wall, terrified. Then, just as suddenly as it had hardened, the pain went. My belly relaxed.

I ran out of the back door. After a few seconds, the pain came back. I could not move. But I had to get help.

I screamed, there on the dust road, in the darkness of night, I screamed.

Then I fainted.

"Thandi," someone called from far away. I heard this, but I was so afraid to open my eyes, I pretended to be unconscious to fool the pain.

"Thandi," I turned on my back and looked up into the soft morning, just before the sun came up, when the world is quiet and in waiting.

It was my sister, my wonderful eldest sister, looking down into my face. She had come to save me.

Then we heard someone else coming. It was Xolokwa, her husband, who had also come to help. He picked me up and carried me through the back door into my little room. There he lay me down gently. He left me there and went out of the hut, for men will become unlucky in worldly matters if they see a birth. The only way, in my custom, bad luck could be avoided is, to rub your eyes with charcoal. There was no charcoal, for the fire had not been lit. So Xolokwa left the room.

The midwife arrived soon afterwards. Her services were free. To her it did not matter that the mother was not married. Her job was to see that both mother and baby were safe. Somehow my pain got less when she came. She told me how to bear down into the pain. I did this naturally, as if I had been taught how to do it.

She told me how to breathe between pains, how to lift my bum slightly, how to push all my strength through bended knees into my heels. My feet were planted wide apart.

The midwife spoke to me softly, gently making me stand up, and led me to stand in the corner of the room. There she made me squat down, showing me how to bear down into the earth in the manner of my ancestors, allowing the contractions to lead the way.

At last, when I was too exhausted to care, too tired to know what was happening, the baby came. It came when the sun was high. It came into the heat of a summer's day in my beloved country, South Africa. I was almost unconscious.

Then it cried. And life laughed. I heard and sank back into the comfort of sleep.

"Sar-key," a familiar voice called. I saw his brown head of curls and red beard, above white teeth with their permanent smile.

I hallucinated into the softness of exhaustion.

The Husband

The big city was kind to me. It covered my shame with anonymity, as cities do, to keep their social fabric intact. But my culture would not allow itself to become part of that fabric. There was no other way for me to keep being respectable amongst my people, in our time, if I did not have a husband. I had to get married. And any husband would do.

It fell to Bithathe and Xolokwa to arrange a marriage for me. Time was running out and the soldier who had caused the family's shame had not come back, Bithathe told the *Kaptein*, who said to her, "If your father and your brother had been alive, they would have deserted Thandi. That is the custom!"

Bithathe said she could not say anything. But there was no way she would move away and leave me alone. Leaving me behind would mean that Hendrick might throw me out of his house.

Instead, she spoke with Anna Catharina. Anna Catharina was very ill and she was having difficulty feeding her baby. Bithathe came up with a very good plan.

"Anna Catharina," she said. She had called her to come and talk with us, and we three women were sitting around the table in the kitchen. My baby was sleeping in the room behind us, and I automatically reached for Anna Catharina's baby.

It happened almost naturally. The baby smelt my milk and snuggled its head into my breast, following the smell. Both women laughed.

"I see you do not have much milk," Bithathe said to Anna Catharina. "Perhaps it might be a good idea if Saartjie shared her milk with both babies."

It was settled. From that day, I became a wet nurse to Anna Catharina's baby. The babies took turns feeding from me.

Because I became a wet nurse to his baby, Hendrick could not tell me to leave. This saved me from a worse fate, because if they had put me out, I would have had to go and live as a slave somewhere else. Worse still, and more likely, the baby and I would both have died of starvation, because I would not have been able to survive on the coast in Cape Town. That is, if some wild animals did not get to me first from around the forests on the hills of the mountains.

I had started to lose faith in Paddy as well. It was the sixth day after the birth of my baby, and there had been no word from him. I felt sure that he must, by now, know about my baby. It was as Bithathe had said: Paddy did not care.

"He is no man for you," Bithathe kept saying to me. "He is not from our people. When trouble comes, they run back to their own lands," my sister said sarcastically.

I did not believe this to be true, that Paddy could not face up to his responsibilities. But what was I to believe? He did not come, and I started to doubt if he ever even liked me.

Then Xolokwa brought a man for me. I was shocked when I saw the old man he brought as my future husband. The most I could say for him is that he had dressed up for the occasion.

He was very old. Very old and gnarled. A shiny, sunburnt, bald scalp shone between sparse tufts of pure white hair. He was a small man with a chipped skin. He looked like a snake. His face was so creased that his eyes could hardly see through their flat slits. He had no facial hair.

"Good, good, good, good," he muttered all the time, under his breath, spit dripping through the gap where his front teeth should have been.

Around his neck he wore so much dry sheep's gut that the little *doit* which hung underneath could hardly be seen. He must have bartered cattle at a great loss for the small Dutch copper coin.

They agreed that no bride price need be paid for me, for I was soiled.

Bithathe and I discussed the future well into that night. She was sad for me, now that she knew what the future husband was like. It would be better, she now felt, if Paddy and I could have lived together.

"It is better that a child be taught by its own father," she said, but she had no power to change custom.

Themba

The name-giving ceremony took place two days later.

I did not look forward to it. My heart was heavy, for I knew that arrangements had been made for me to get married and leave to go back to the eastern Cape as soon as the ceremony was over. There was no celebration planned.

Very early that morning, before the first bird called, I wrapped my baby in my warmest *kaross.* I slipped quietly out of the back door and ran down to the river. By the time the sun's first knives reflected over the water, I was walking through the trees with my baby.

After a short while, I came to a little copse. There I lay my baby down carefully on a patch of grass. I went to sit next to her, facing the mound of stone.

I prayed to my Tata. I was in the presence of one of the graves of my ancestors, and we prayed to our ancestors in times of trouble.

"When you feel weak, go inside yourself," I heard Tata say, as he often told us. Look inside. You will find strength there.

I remembered a day under a great tree, with Tata. It had been very hot. I was still very young. My father had allowed me to go into the veld with him that day, and I was glad. It meant that I would not spend the day helping to collect firewood and preparing food. It was one of my earliest memories. I had a glorious time running behind Tata, chasing butterflies and swatting flies, because they droned and made the sun lazy. The sun would not move from its place right in the middle of the sky and it had become very hot.

Tata had gone to sit under a tree and I had sat with him. I remembered the great sadness coming from Tata, for my mama had died not too long before that. I had snuggled into Tata's chest and he cradled me.

"Why is Tata crying?" I asked.

Tata answered my question with a question. "Why did you pull your little brother's ear this morning?" he asked.

I remember smiling. I did not like my baby brother in those days. It was his fault that my mama no longer came home. Since he had arrived, my mama had never come to sleep in the hut any longer. I had not seen my mama since my younger brother had come. When I was alone with my brother, I liked to make him cry. It took away some of my anger against him in those days, before I started to love him.

And since my brother had come, Tata was always sad. I felt his sadness all the time.

"Little one," my father said, hugging me to his chest, "never forget. Inside, you are strong. You have vital force, like the river, like the trees." This Tata repeated to us many times, in many ways.

I sat there that morning next to the grave of my ancestor, and pleaded with Tata to send his spirit to melt into mine, to make it much stronger.

Then I picked up my child carefully and walked back to the house, to face my future.

The baby girl was given the great name of my father, together with the great name of my mother. The Khoikhoi believed in treating all boys and girls the same. We called her Themba for short.

We rubbed little Themba with buchu[73] powder.

"Thy name be Xamnubus," from my mother's side, because her cheeks were brown, puffed and soft, "Pades," in honour of her natural father, Paddy, "daughter of Thandi," the *Kaptein* solemnised that day. "We shall call you Themba," he said with a short smile.

I took my baby, and I wished that I could just stand there with her, and that life would never change. I knew that as soon as I put baby down, my life would change forever.

And my life did change, but not in the way that I had feared.

A commotion started up outside. The dogs started barking, and excited voices floated into the house. As was the custom, everyone else had remained outside during the name-giving ceremony.

We looked towards the backdoor, and I saw the stranger.

"Paddy!" I cried. I lifted Themba and burst into joyful sobs.

In amazement, Paddy reached for his baby as the others left the room. Themba stared into her father's face. It was the first time that she had opened her eyes completely. Soft brown eyes stared through thick, almost black eyelashes into the hazel eyes of her father. The baby reached out a podgy hand and curled her little fingers around Paddy's finger, which she brought to her mouth immediately.

She already showed signs of the beauty which was to be hers. Paddy brought her up to his face as if to kiss her, but changed his mind. It looked like her chocolate cheeks were powdered over with a pink blush, the shade of the sky when the sun has gone down into a blue sea on a cloudless day. She looked small and beautiful. Paddy could not kiss her with his rough beard. Instead, he lay his hand on her head and gently fondled her velvety light-brown curls. He sighed happily.

I stood waiting patiently behind Paddy. I was waiting to be noticed. The joy I felt at the sight of father and daughter together was too big for words.

Paddy could not take his eyes off his daughter.

"Her nose is the same shape as yours, Thandi," he said and the joy ran over my cup of happiness, for he had called me by my birth name!

He held his arm out to me. I shyly allowed him to bring me into a circle with my baby.

He did not hand Themba back to me.

Grief

I do not remember too well what happened with my husband to be. In a way I felt sorry for him, but then I thought he deserved to be deserted, wanting to marry a young girl like me. And if he, as old as he was, could not give me another child, then, as was our custom, I would have been taken by one of his younger male relatives to keep the line of the family strong. I shuddered when I thought of this, that his family is probably as ugly as he is. I was happy to have been saved from that fate.

Xolokwa sent for the old man. Bithathe was there with them outside at the back of the house. I was sitting inside the room and could hear everything they said.

"This is not how things should be done," Xolokwa said, without direct apology. "This is a bad way. I do not agree. I am not happy," he said.

The old man listened to the news in the way that only older people can, with an inner shrug. His marriage was not to be. The baby father had returned, and it is very important that the baby stay with mother and father.

I knew that the old man's life shrank a little more from the inside when he heard this, but to him it was just another disappointment. His life would carry on drying out, I thought.

This I knew, for our belief is that nothing can be hastened, nor pushed forward, nor stopped by the Earth, Sun, Wind or Rain. Neither the old man, nor Xolokwa, nor us women, had any control over it. It was his destiny to accept things, as it had been mine.

I was happy. Paddy and I were settled into a little hut which they had put up in *Zoutrivier*[74] for us. This was so that I could be close to Anna Catharina and keep helping her and feeding her baby.

Paddy and Xolokwa built it from river stone in the rectangular Irish way, for Paddy was the architect.

When the single-roomed hut was done, Bithathe and I smeared the floor with cow dung. The good weather helped the floor to dry out within a few days, while Paddy went back to his regiment and I stayed back in the little room of the house.

The months which followed were the happiest time of my life. I lived in the hut with my baby and shared it with Paddy when he could get away from the barracks.

Time flew. It flew on dreams. I spent my days cuddling Themba, crooning to her, inspecting her, checking that all her fingers and toes were still there every day. I kissed her, laughed with her, lived into her every frown, smile, movement, all the time loving and pressing my new creation into my bosom, flesh to flesh in softness and wonderment.

Then life turned with the winds.

The weather had started to go slightly cooler. It was the time when the sun feels sorry for the people many rivers away, when it turns its face to their lands, shedding its warmth on their pale faces. The time when the sun melts away the ice from the lands across the mountains on the other side of the big rivers, many seas away.

It was in the middle of the year, when the brief winter of our country comes just quickly enough to quench the earth's thirst before it leaves again to share the rain with other peoples.

Paddy and I spent our time in our little hut when he had time off. It was dream-time, which coloured everything softly. Even the Cape Town winter weather looked softer to me that year. Everyone else was complaining about the spiteful north westerly winds riding on strong winds and chucking buckets of water into their faces. But that winter left me feeling fresh and light, for the icy sting of the rains was thawed by love.

I carried my baby on my back that Sunday. Paddy and I went for a walk. We loved to walk. One of our favourite walks, a tough one, which we took that day, was next to the ravine between Lion's Head and Table Mountain.

We walked from the northern side to the southern side of the Cape Peninsula, where the southern seas are. We walked through a deep, dry ravine, along the paths made by mountain buck and goats. And then, after a rest on the white beaches on the other side, another long walk back.

We enjoyed it, walking in the shade of the tall pine trees most of the way. We ate wild berries, roots and fruit along the way and drank fresh water from the mountain streams. The tall trees surrounded the long cut in the earth, as we called the ravine. The trees blocked out the sky as we walked between the two mountains. A soft breeze, the breath coming from the nose of the lion mountain, having turned its back on the table mountain behind it, poured down on us.

Later, when my sorrow was very dark, I would remember how a mountain buck had sprung onto our path. It stood, mesmerised, its two fine front ankles pressing down into the earth nervously. As suddenly as it had come, the buck scampered back into the trees, its delicate hind legs arching as it disappeared into the bush. I remembered this afterwards, when my mind was frozen with shock and grief.

The north-westerly wind attacked us when we came back through the mountains. We walked downhill into the town and the wind drove into us so that we had to cling to each other for support.

We ran down into the safety of The Avenue, which runs through Cape Town gardens, a long broad walk. We went to stand under an old tree, laughing and happy.

Themba had become very irritable on my back. She kept crying and would only stop when Paddy put his little finger into her mouth. But she seemed to have no strength to suck on it. She closed her eyes and slept, a restless sleep, her little feet kicking against my back. Soon she would wake up and start crying again.

"It's been a long day for her," Paddy said, and I agreed. "Let's get back," he suggested, and we rushed to get home.

On our way we picked up dry, dead logs of kreupelboom for our evening firewood.

Later, after we had eaten, Paddy told me that he had to go to see Xolokwa and Bithathe. He was going to do a short brotherhood ceremony with Xolokwa, which sealed a lifelong friendship between the two men. He also needed to speak with them, he said.

I did not answer him. I hardly heard him. I had little Themba in my arms. I rocked the restless child back and forth.

I ignored him, for I knew what he was going to see Xolokwa and Bithathe about, and I did not want to hear about it. It was again about me going to Ireland with him. But they did not want me to take Themba with me.

"Thandi, there is no other way," Paddy said. I liked the way he had learnt to say my given name. He pulled out the last part, unlike everyone else, who said it with a long beginning. That night, though, I ignored him.

"Thandi," he said again. He came up to me, cupped my chin in his hand. He lifted my face to his. He came down on his knees so that he could face me and look into my eyes.

"When Themba is older, then we can come back for her," he said. "Xolokwa and Bithathe will not allow us to take her with us. You know that, Thandi."

"Maybe if you ask Bithathe, she might agree," I said. Paddy had asked me many times to go to his country with him. Each time I had said nothing. I wanted to go, yet I was afraid to go and leave my family behind.

"I will speak with Bithathe," he promised, and he left.

What I did not know was that he had been told to leave on the next ship for England.

I tried to soothe little Themba while Paddy was gone. She was now crying really hard. No matter what I did, I could not get her to quieten down. I was worried. I walked around inside the hut, singing softly to her, rocking her back and forth. But Themba would not stop crying.

And she was burning with fever. I had to do something.

In a panic, I ran over to the hut in which Bithathe and Xolokwa were living.

"Bithathe! Paddy!" They jumped up and Bithathe took baby from me. Themba was taking shallow, gasping little breaths.

"I'll take her to the army hospital," Paddy said immediately. The only hospital at that time was the one next to the castle. The hospital was there only for the soldiers, but Themba was his baby, and they would see to her, I knew. But I could not allow this. It was not our custom.

"No!" I said.

I was to carry the guilt of my refusal with me forever.

But Bithathe and Xolokwa agreed with me. They also did not want the baby to go to the white people's doctor.

"Go and call the healer," Bithathe told Xolokwa.

The healer lived behind St Stephen's Church in the Malay quarter in *Bokaap*. It is on the slopes of Signal Hill, the rump of the Lion. Xolokwa had to run uphill from *Zoutrivier*, all the way up the lower high street, up into Kortmarkstraat. He ran fast, in a panic, while Paddy and Bithathe and I wrapped Themba in wet skins.

Xolokwa came back with the healer on a little wagon.

By that time Themba was hardly breathing.

The healer reached for Themba while we stood by. His slowness made me want to scream. He smeared raw sheep's fat all over my baby. Then, from the paraphernalia hanging around his neck, he took a closed seashell. Carefully, breathing gently onto the shell with eyes closed, he slowly prized it opened. I knew that the shell contained a powder made from the dry leaves of the *buchu* plant, which grows on the slopes of the mountain, mixed with urine. Only men's urine could be used, for women's urine does not heal.

He muttered to himself all the time, working very slowly.

Paddy was getting frantic. The healer seemed to know what he was doing, but Paddy knew he was not a doctor, and I could see by the look on his face that he did not trust the healer.

Themba was turning blue and hardly breathing at all.

"Don't you think—" Paddy started.

"Shhh!" Everyone shut him up together. The healer was not to be disturbed.

Paddy watched. I could see he was becoming more and more agitated, for he was sweating with impatience. The healer slowly took out a sharp knife. He was about to shave Themba's head.

He looked down in baby's face, I looked too.

Themba had stopped breathing. I could not take it in.

For a long time, the healer just held his hand over Themba's eyes, while we stood, the men with bowed heads, Bithathe and I holding back our cries behind fists pressed tightly against our lips.

Finally, the healer solemnly smeared my baby's little *kaross* with *buchu* powder and anointed it with fat and water. He rolled the *kaross* around her. Then he handed the dead child to her father.

He left us without a word. Also without payment. Payment would have been given in the form of a feast, but only if the treatment was successful.

The wail which escaped from me was so intense that my hot tears felt like blood squeezed out of an open wound inside me.

I wept until I had no tears left.

A Family Decision

Bithathe arranged a cleansing ceremony for my baby, as was our custom.

Then Themba, my baby, our baby, was buried in the same way that Tata was buried. But unlike Tata, she was easy to curl up like a baby in the womb, because she had not been long out of it.

Bithathe put her in a small *kaross* made of baby lamb skin and sewed her in with cow gut. Then they placed her in a tiny hole, sitting upright, before closing it up with earth. The little mound was not far away from the heap where I had prayed to my ancestors not too long ago.

I had lost the most precious thing in my life. My life now had no direction left.

It was easier for me then to agree with Paddy that I would go to the land of England, and that he would come and fetch me.

"It's not far from Dublin to London, Thandi," he said. "Just a short journey across the sea. The big army ships take just a few hours, and I will be there to fetch you back home with me." He was standing in his uniform, looking smart with white trousers and scarlet tunic, when he said this. He looked very smart and handsome.

I agreed. But the family had to agree too.

So they held counsel to decide if I should go away. The whole family and everyone who was important came to discuss whether I should go to the far land of England. Usually white men were not allowed to attend counsel. But because Paddy had sealed a brotherhood with Xolokwa, Paddy was now part of our family, and he attended counsel with us. But he did not say anything, for it was the elders who made these big decisions.

Even if Hendrick was by then a free man, he could sit in counsel, because we are still one people. It did not make a difference if you were free or unfree.

I was keen that they agree that I go. It would mean that I would see a new land, with different people. I would go to enjoy a new life. I would have new hope.

Usually only the men were allowed to hold counsel together, while the women and children sit on the outside of the circle of men. But that day it was different. Everyone sat behind the little house, women and children included. It was late afternoon and the sound of the *Zoutrivier*, my beloved river, could be heard in the background over the satisfied drone of the earth.

Our *Kaptein* had come too. It was an important decision, which could not be made without the chief. He did not say anything. He watched quietly because he would speak only if the men did not agree. He was holding his cane in front of him. His cane had a copper head. His two bodyguards were standing behind him.

Serious business such as this was always discussed with long silences. Each man sat upright, never speaking when someone else was speaking, especially when the speaker was old with white hair.

"Two years, that is all," Hendrick had said.

"Khoi never leave their families!" my young brother interrupted. But he was not given a chance to speak further. He had spoken out of turn, had interrupted Hendrick, who was older. The other men grunted. He dropped his eyes and went quiet.

Bithathe was also there that day with Xolokwa. "It will be good for you, Thandi," she whispered to me during a silence.

"Go and forget what has happened," Bithathe said quietly. "Also, wait for Paddy. He is a soldier, a good man. He will come back for you." I felt good. It was good to hear Bithathe say that about Paddy. She had started to really like Paddy and that made my life easier.

"You must look after her," the *Kaptein* said sternly to Paddy. All eyes turned to Paddy. He nodded very seriously. He was sitting on the outskirts. I could see that he was uncomfortable, because he kept standing up to stretch his legs. All the other men were sitting comfortably on their haunches. He did try to copy them but could not do it for long.

"Thandi is our own. You must make sure she is safe!" Paddy put his palms together and bowed his head to our *Kaptein*, and I was very proud of him.

It was agreed that I would bring the money back to them, the money which I was to get from being a nursery maid in England, where they pay much money to nursery maids like me. I promised my family that I would give them half the money I made.

"That is agreed," our *Kaptein* said, and everything was settled.

"So long as she does not let our people down!" This came from an old aunt, who suddenly stood up and spat for emphasis over the heads of the young boys in front of her. At the same time the *Kaptein* stood up, and her stream of spit, brown with tobacco, landed next to his stick.

It was agreed.

I was happy-sad. I was going to see the big world, but I was going to leave my family behind. I was going to miss them very much, I knew. But then I always wanted to sail across the seas. I'd been longing to go on one of the big ships which regularly stopped in Cape Town harbour. When sitting on the rocks at the foot of the mountain, I had for hours dreamt of being on one of them, enjoyed watching them sail into Tafelbaai. They looked so graceful on top of the blue-green waters, moving without effort, like swans.

I would be very important. Everyone would come and say goodbye to me.

Plus, I was going to be rich.

And Paddy would come from far away Ireland to fetch me.[75]

The End

For students who would like to read more about Saartjie, I have set out in the following pages my thoughts on how I feel history could have written her story, and why I think that Saartjie was powerless but to make the decisions she made.

Monica Clarke

Epilogue

Saartjie died[76] in Paris on 29th December 1815.[77] In February the next year, the French Police received a letter from the scientist, Etienne Geoffroy Saint Hilaire, who worked with Cuvier (who did the autopsy after Saartjie's death),[78] in which he asked Monsieur Boucheseiche, head of the Paris police, permission to take Saartjie's body back to the Jardin des Plantes (Jardin du Rois) for an autopsy.[79]

The body was too coarse to feel the utmost of our sorrows and our joys.
Therefore, we abandoned it as rubbish:
We left it below us to march forward, a breathing simulacrum,
On its own unaided level,
Subject to influences from which in normal times our instincts have shrunk.[80]

Tribute to a Grandmother

Ouma[81] Saartjie, you were put on display because you had a big bottom. But the Cape Town of 1807 did not find anything unusual in the size of your buttocks. Neither would the Cape Town of today. It was only when you went to Europe that your shape caused excitement. Your buttocks were obese, but under outer clothing there was nothing remarkable about you. It was only in Europe that your *steatopygia,*[82] as the scientists call a big bottom, or the shelf-like protuberances as Laurens van der Post described them,[83] caused a stir. Hendrick Cezars invited them to feel your posterior parts.[84] And they did.

Why was this?

It is because the Europeans saw what they wanted to see. The sexual organs of us Africans, men and women, have for centuries been a curiosity to them. They wanted to have a peep at your private parts, each person wanting to confirm their suspicions for themselves. The 'Hottentot' as they called us, was reputedly the missing link[85] between man and ape, a sexual icon,[86] with sexual organs which took on gross proportions in the mind of the European. Thus they came to gawk at you, to confirm their preconceptions about you and our people, and their 'eyes saw no more than their minds, shaped at home, were prepared to accept.'[87]

Alexander Dunlop, a medical doctor, knew of this curious pre-occupation with the genitalia of the Khoikhoen and played on it. Together with Hendrick Cezars and the other exhibitors, they turned a natural phenomenon into a commercial spectacle. When it backfired, they shifted the shame and blame onto you, and you, a gullible young woman, were quite defenceless against their influence and unable to refute their opinions of us.

The historians say that when you exhibited your body, you were driven by greed, that you insisted on making a spectacle of yourself for money, and that you collaborated in your own degradation.[88] For almost two hundred years after that last day in the Royal Courts of Justice in Fleet Street, London, the world has believed that you were the author of your own doom, that you deserved your lot.

I cry when I hear it said that you knew full well that you were not travelling afar 'to remain just a domestic servant; no one got rich from that'.[89] I cry for you, for this is exactly what you believed when you left South Africa. Of course you did expect to make money. And you did expect to become rich. But the richness which you were talking about was not the richness of some others, Saartjie. You did not have the ability, resources, nor expertise, to measure money, or its worth, in their way. It is our kind of rich, where having a family, a caring community and a quality of life in abundance means more than money in the bank. You did expect to be able to enrich your family and your community in that way with the money you were going to take home to them. All of us migrant, immigrant workers send money home so our people can enjoy the benefits of our 'riches'.

If one looks at the objections which poured in from the British public against the exhibition, then it is clear that the British people cared about you, Saartjie. You thought they were a good people. I think so too, and I can understand why you rather liked being in their country with them. They wrote to the newspapers that you were under threat of physical violence, that you were frightened, that you acted under coercion.[90]

You left our country as an ordinary, curious, young woman. You travelled to a foreign country with all the excitement and expectation of any young adult, wanting to see the big world, eager to make some money. What's wrong with that? Even today—if only you could see what appears on television and in magazines—there is nothing unusual about the idea of displaying your person. Your showing yourself is not the moral issue it has been made out to be by your critics, then and now. You showed her body without shame. And you waited for your wages without guilt.

You did it so that people from other lands could see, and to hear, what our people are like. The Geographical Society (1830) had not yet been founded, so there was as yet no international scientific network which shared knowledge. Ethnology, the study of human peoples, was in its early stages, and scientists said that they needed 'raw material' of different people, animals and plants to study, to make copies of, and to discuss at their symposia.[91]

This is why the showmen who organised, what is now known as freak shows, claimed that they were making a valuable contribution to science by putting their 'specimens' on show.[92]

There is no doubt that Alexander Dunlop, a medical man, would, through Hendrick Cezars, have given you and your family these plausible reasons to convince you that to exhibit your person is a good thing. Hendrick Cezars, being a freed slave himself, would have influenced our family to let you go. He surely told them that you would be able to speak up for our people and culture, as did some of our famous ancestors.

You believed all of them, Saartjie.

I do not.

I believe that Alexander Dunlop used his position as a man of medicine to cover up his real motive, which was to display you as a piece of erotic meat, to wet base appetites and lust and to appeal to the sordid mentality of the Georgian mind.[93] And to make money out of you.

You wanted to entertain people, you did not find anything wrong with that. Nor do I. You even took your *ramkie,* a little guitar made from the lower half of a calabash[94] along to entertain people with. Entertaining foreign people is an enjoyable form of paying social respect. I have read how you were 'magnificently attired' and gave guests gifts[95] (although personally I doubt that you had any gifts to give!)

I'm sure you knew about, and would have wanted to follow, our ancestors who left our country to go and entertain people overseas. It is part of our history to do so. Hundreds of years before your birth, some of our forefathers had done so and had returned safely to our homeland. For example, Cory, who travelled to England in 1613 and returned safely the next year.[96] And, of course, Herry the Interpreter, who travelled to Bantam (now Jakarta) on an English ship forty years later.[97]

You could not read, so you would not have known that another one of our ancestors, called 'A Hottentot of

Distinction', living in London during your mother's time, in 1750, wrote in a letter to his friend at the Cape of Good Hope of how much he enjoyed dancing, singing, and 'playing on all manner of instruments with the Europeans'.[98]

Your decision to do the same was influenced by such much-admired ancestors in our past. But instead of the enjoyment you expected to give and receive, they came to poke and pinch your body. And to test whether your buttocks were natural, the point of a parasol was dug into your behind.[99]

Those things you could not have expected.

You believed the promises of Alexander Dunlop and Hendrick Cezars. When Dunlop said that he would return you safely home after two years, would pay your passage home, you believed him.[100] He also offered to the court that he would secure an annuity for life under a trustee.[101] The court believed him. Why should you have doubted him?

As it happened, you never received the money, half the profits from the exhibition you were promised. The money went from Hendrick, to his wife Anna Catharina. And eventually Pieter Cezars got the money through Hendrick's estate.[102] Your return fare home was never paid. Neither did Dunlop ever set up a trust fund for you as he had promised to do. Neither the court, the Attorney General, nor any of the abolitionists ever forced him to make good his promises.

You stuck to your side of the deal, Saartjie. Until you died in Paris four years after arriving in England, you stuck to your deal. You died still waiting for the money, still believing that you were going to be sent home. You died alone, away from your family, with no friends around you. You never saw the father of your dead child, the drummer, again. You never saw our country, South Africa, again.

You were the object of many jokes, cartoons[103] and insulting street songs.[104] Even South Africa had unfortunately adopted one such cartoon as its official recognition of you for many years.[105] Thank God they changed this in 2002.[106]

History says that you arrived in Paris on 18th September 1814.[107] If your plight was difficult in Britain, it was worse in France. You were on display in Paris, pinched and poked for between 5, and 12 hours a day.[108] This time your keeper was an animal showman. That must have been awful for you, Saartjie. My heart bled when I read that you shared lodgings with Reaux's animals at 7 Courdes Fontaines (now Place de Valois).[109]

The French public enjoyed the spectacle. By this time you were quite ill, but you remained on display throughout. Your various illnesses are said to have ranged from an inflammatory and eruptive sickness, boils, catarrh, pleurisy, dropsy of the breast and smallpox.[110] You poor woman. An animal keeper was not likely to have found medical help for you. No wonder you took to the bottle.

More cartoons followed in the same way as they had in London, in newspapers and on billboards. A month before your death, a popular play about you had a successful run in Paris, a vaudeville in one act.[111]

But not a whisper of complaint seemed to escape from your lips through all this, Saartjie.

And now your lips are forever sealed.

And I want you to know that I believe that you were much too stubborn to have taken your loincloth off without much argument. You were by that time quite ill. You would not have taken your cloth off easily. In fact, I suspect that the writer who said that they discovered your *sinus pudoris* only after your death, might have been right.[112]

Your private parts were your pain, your punishment. People had come to stare at you, to insult you, for a glimpse of your genitals. You knew that, Saartjie. They tried to see what the reputed vaginal flap of the Hottentot woman looked like, they tried to see whether your female parts could prove what Captain Cook had written about.[113] They, the public, scientists, as well as medics, believed, like the 17th century medical authority Nicholas Culpepper, that 'the bigger the clitoris in a woman, the more lustful they are.'[114] They wanted you to be the proof, but you would not let them see.

They came to feed their sexual fantasies, to see for themselves whether it is true that once a man had slept with an African woman, he would never be able to sleep with a white woman again,[115] and vice versa.

I can tell you, Saartjie, that this racist belief of the contamination which results from carnal knowledge of a black person has remained so strong, over the centuries, that it was at the core of apartheid South Africa's Immorality Act, which forbade sex between white and black.

And your dreams were true. After your death, the scientists claimed you as their own. First in the Jardin de Plantes in Paris, your body was taken for dissection.[116] They sawed your skull open and cut out your brain. Then they sliced out your genitals. After that, they pulled out your anus. They made wax moulds of all those soft parts. Your skin was most probably also ripped off your body, for your skin was not with your other body parts in the *Musee de l'homme* in Paris. The stuffed skin of a 'Hottentot' woman which turned up in

Britain in 1850, seen by Robert Knox, the Scottish anatomist, was in probability your skin.[117]

They left such insulting opinions behind about you, that I am ashamed to write them down. They said that your movements were like those of a monkey; that you had a habit of protruding your lips like an orang-outang and compared your buttocks to the swollen genitals of a female monkey during menstruation.[118] Having had their say, the scientists took your skeleton, made a plaster cast of it, and placed the remaining you in the *Musee de l'Homme* in Paris. Just as in your dream, Saartjie, they put you in a glass case marked with a number 33.

I'm so sorry, Saartjie.

Those people knew nothing, wanted to know nothing about the real you, Saartjie. You, the woman, the mother, the daughter of a nation known for its honesty and love of peace,[119] the real you, remains unknown to them. They did not even bother to find out what your real name was.

Yet history believes their stories about you.

Your character and your motives have been the offensive guesswork of scientists and academics for hundreds of years. Upper class, middle class, mostly white male academics have claimed your physiology and motives as their private domain. They drew their insulting opinions from myth, then entrenched them as scientific fact. And it is with the ink of their opinions that your history has been written. To them you will remain the 'Hottentot savage', the alcoholic[120] prostitute, who courted her own degradation to earn money.[121]

And all that stuff they believed about you in court! How could the court case have been impartial, when the person who had started it all, the army surgeon Alexander Dunlop, was himself present when you were questioned? When even the court was grateful to him for attending the ?[122] Yes, Dunlop, your persecutor was there, despite Justice le Blanc's express instructions that the examination take place in the absence of the animal keeper himself, and of every person in his employ. Dunlop did not regard himself as the animal keeper. In fact he said that Hendrick Cezars had been removed from his position as exhibitor. They lied, lied, lied.

I do believe that Hendrick and the doctor had lots of time to prepare you for the examination, that they threatened you to say what you said, because, and this you would not know, Saartjie, but a month before the court hearing, on 17th October of the same year 1810, the Attorney General had tried to bring the same matter before the same court. He did not succeed.[123] Reasons for this were never given.

The fact that he had tried to bring the same matter to court twice was never even discussed, although it was mentioned in court.

The first abortive hearing was just what Dunlop and Cezars needed, so they could prepare themselves to win again, which they did and did very well by grooming you to go along with them. They knew, for more than a month that the matter of your release from exhibition would be brought back to the courts.

They had plenty of time to take you through the rehearsals of your answers, while threatening you and tiring you out physically, mentally, emotionally and spiritually. You were living with them at No 1 York Street, London all the time. Dunlop told William Bullock this himself.[124] They even had time to remove Hendrick from the exhibition before the hearing in November, to show how benevolent they were towards you, to show that you were no longer under any threat.[125]

What a pity none of this was explained to the court.

You were coerced. You were afraid. You were under restraint all the time, throughout the exhibition and during the examination.

Many people who had seen the exhibition spoke out in the newspapers. They said you were displayed as a chained beast under restraint. They told of how Cezars clenched his fist at you, in a menacing posture, which was confirmed by Cezars' own counsel in court.[126]

One man, who described himself as An Englishman, wrote that Cezars had held up a stick to you, like a wild beast keeper, to intimidate you into obedience.[127] Another said that Cezars treated you like a dog,[128] and Hendrick himself said that you are sick and sulky. "Always sulky when there is company there." Hendrick called you a wild beast, then took a long piece of bamboo and shook it at you. After this, the man said, you immediately obeyed Hendrick, doing what he wanted you to do, which was to play on your guitar, which you had not wanted to do, because you were very ill by then.[129]

Alexander Dunlop regarded you as a thing, his property.[130]

The Court failed you, Saartjie, when it found that you were under no threat of danger. Lord Ellenborough, the Judge, thought that the removal of Hendrick Cezars from the exhibition automatically meant that you were safe, that you were being well treated.[131] We know that this was not so.

And we also know that you were forced to collude with your oppressors.

Now we shall never hear what it is you really wanted to say.

I cannot understand why the court found that there was nothing indecent about the exhibition, that the laws of morality permitted such an exhibition. This, despite reports that the exhibition was 'base to the extreme',[132] and disgraceful both to decency and humanity.

All else failing, I think that Cezars and Dunlop should have been brought before the courts for fraud. They had forced you to 'sign' an agreement which you could not understand, because you could not read.

The agreement was dated 29th October 1810, when you were already in England. (This was just after the first abortive court hearing).

They claim that you said that you were a domestic servant of Alexander Dunlop from March of that year. They changed the length of the contract to six years and made you say that you had personally attended the Governor of the Cape of Good Hope, where the agreement had been ratified.[133]

The agreement must have been read over to you by a Notary Public, Officer of the Court, in England. But how could you have understood him if he was an Englishman who could not speak your language? I can see you standing there, scared, between the three men, nodding your terrified agreement, not understanding.

The whole agreement is a confused nonsense. It could not have been ratified in Cape Town as it was signed in England in front of a Notary Public long after you had left Cape Town. The contract was not for six years, but for two years. Dunlop had told William Bullock this. Hendrick said it too.[134]

But regardless of the contents of the agreement, it was void. It could have had no effect, because the law did not recognise agreements with the Khoikhoen, who were regarded as incapable to enter into agreements, unless this was done in the presence of a Magistrate. The Attorney General himself told the court this.[135]

And, most importantly, the permission of the Governor of the Cape, Lord Caledon, had never been obtained.[136] This was totally against the law. When they removed you from the Cape, Saartjie, they were guilty of a crime.

I do not believe that you ever intended to live in Europe permanently, Saartjie. You were brought up to believe that one is safe only for so long as you are in your place of birth and when you leave it, you are in danger.[137]

I have no doubt that history would have told a better tale about you if the black leaders had been consulted. There were in excess of 10,000 black people in Britain at the beginning of the 19th century.[138] And according to the Gentleman's Magazine, by 1764 there were an estimated 20,000 blacks living in London alone. [139]They made up a large, militant community, especially in London. They are known for retaliating ill-treatment, provoking respect from whites, and for keeping their own self-esteem intact. They were in the army, they were in the navy. They were self-employed. Many of them were educated through the Sunday schools. Their social commitment was to care for people like you, Saartjie, who had newly arrived and were 'adrift in the alien world of London.'[140] And they were not passive and subservient in their roles, but gathered together for collective security, care for their collective interests, pursue independent social life and to safeguard their own wellbeing. The organised their own exclusive social events; gathered together in private houses; attended slave cases in large numbers; raised money for blacks in distress and cultivated important political ties with prominent white sympathisers and abolitionists.

Amongst them were some prominent people. Some of them were your direct neighbours in London, did you know that, Saartjie? For example, the famous slave Equiano, who visited with Thomas Hardy as house guest in Piccadilly and Ottobach Cugoano, a slave who wrote a treatise of the slave trade's evils in 1787.[141] These leaders should have been consulted, but they were not. They should have spoken with you, but you never met them. But did you never even hear about them, Saartjie? They should have been brought to court to speak up for you, but they were not.

Saartjie, you started your life as a lover of laughter, in the true meaning of Venus. But you died scorned, unlike the Roman Goddess of Love. Instead, you are immortalised as a Lover of Genitals and a Goddess of Sexual Desire, like Aphrodite, the Venus of the Greeks.[142]

For over 200 years, your body was regarded 'too course to feel the utmost of our sorrows and our joys' and was, therefore, abandoned as rubbish.[143] This is no longer so. You have at last been rescued out of the 'clutches of imperialism'.[144]

I am proud to be one of your descendants. I am sorry that I could not be there with the thousands of our family who lay you to your proper rest in Hankey, South Africa, near the banks of your favourite Gamtoos River on 9th August 2002.[145]

I bow to you, Ouma Saartjie, our Grandmother.

Monica Clarke

Who were the KhoiKhoi?

Why did Saartjie's people, the KhoiKhoi, call themselves *'First People'*—*'People of People'*—*'Men of Men'?*

According to <u>South African History Online</u> "The Khoikhoi brought a new way of life to South Africa and to the San, who were hunter-gatherers as opposed to herders. This led to misunderstandings and subsequent conflict between the two groups."

In around 2300 BP (Before Present), hunter-gatherers called the San acquired domestic stock in what is now modern day Botswana. Their population grew, and spread throughout the Western half of South Africa. They were the first pastoralists in southern Africa, and called themselves Khoikhoi (or Khoe), which means 'men of men' or 'the real people'. This name was chosen to show pride in their past and culture. The Khoikhoi brought a new way of life to South Africa and to the San, who were hunter-gatherers as opposed to herders. This led to misunderstandings and subsequent conflict between the two groups.

The Khoikhoi were the first native people to come into contact with the Dutch settlers in the mid 17th century. As the Dutch took over land for farms, the Khoikhoi were dispossessed, exterminated, or enslaved and therefore their numbers dwindled. The Khoikhoi were called the 'Hottentots' by European settlers because the sound of their language was so different from any European language, and they could not pronounce many of the words and sounds.

The Khoikhoi used a word while dancing that sounded like 'Hottentots' and therefore settlers referred to the Khoikhoi by this name—however today this term is considered derogatory. The settlers used the term 'Bushmen' for the San, a term also considered derogatory today. Many of those whom the colonists called 'Bushmen' were in fact Khoikhoi or former Khoikhoi. For this reason, scholars sometimes find it convenient to refer to hunters and herders together as 'Khoisan'.

When European settlement began, Khoikhoi groups called the Namaqua were settled in modern day Namibia and the north-eastern Cape; others, including the Korana, along the Orange River; and the Gonaqua, interspersed among the Xhosa in the Eastern Cape. But the largest concentration of Khoikhoi, numbering in the tens of thousands inhabited the well-watered pasture lands of the south-western Cape. These 'Cape' Khoikhoi would be the first African population to bear the brunt of White settlement.

Nomadic Heritage

The Khoikhoi kept herds of animals such as goat, cattle and sheep and had to move around to find enough grazing land for their animals. They moved according to the seasons and only stayed in one place for a few weeks. This meant that they had to be able to carry all their belongings themselves, or load them onto the backs of their animals.

Houses had to be very light and easy to erect and take apart. For this reason, they were made of thin poles covered with reed mats. Even pots and buckets were made of wood with small handles to make them easier to tie to animals' backs. They also wore clothes made of leather, like the San.

The animals, especially cattle, were a sign of wealth and the Khoikhoi only ate cattle that had died or had been stolen from their enemies. They only killed their own animals for important occasions like funerals or weddings. The women milked the animals and gathered wild plants from the veld and the men killed game for everyday food. This shows that the Khoikhoi hunted and gathered, but also herded animals.

Khoikhoi Society and Language

Khoikhoi society consisted of both rich and poor, as animals—which were a sign of wealth—could belong to individuals. This is because animals provided food, clothes and transport. This was completely different from the San, who were all considered equal and shared everything. Wealthier Khoikhoi people would share their milk with poorer members of their group, but would still be considered more important. They would also rub animal fat over their bodies to show their wealth.

Khoisan languages, characterised by implosive consonants or 'clicks', belonged to a totally different language family from those of the Bantu speakers. In contrast to the San who spoke highly divergent languages, the Khoikhoi spoke closely related dialects of the same language. NÁ má, previously called Hottentot, is the most populous and widespread of the Khoikhoi and San languages. It belongs to the Khoe language family, and is spoken in Namibia,

Botswana, and South Africa by the Namaqua, Damara, and Hai'om, as well as smaller ethnic groups such as the Khomani (to read more about the language see the history of the San).

The Kora

The Korana or Kora were a nomadic Khoikhoi group that probably derived their name from a chief called Kora (or Gora), who was originally a leader of the Gorachouqua (`-qua' meaning 'people of'). This leader detached himself from this group with his followers and became the first great chief of the Korana. Others say that the name Korana could mean 'the real thing'.

Initially there were two main groups, the Great Korana and the Little Korana. Each of these broke into splinter groups that divided until there were many groups whose names have been slowly forgotten or were not recorded. Quarrels over water and grazing rights, or the ownership of women or livestock usually caused the divisions amongst groups. When parties split up, they usually assumed the name of their leader. But sometimes they took the name of a place where they had stayed for a long time.

One such case was the name Hoogekraal ('High Kraal'), the original name for Pacaltsdorp, near George. Korana family names tended to signify a special characteristic or occupation such as the Towenaars (Sorcerers) and the Regshande (Right-handers). Where the first Chief Kora lived is unknown, but in early times, most Korana lived near the Gariep, Vaal and Harts rivers and others moved into the Overberg and the Karoo.

The last great Korana trek took place during the late 17th century, when they trekked from their chiefdoms in the south-western Cape to escape pressure from White settlers. These Korana trekkers travelled along the western trading routes as far north as the great river that they called Gariep, which means 'river'. The early pioneers added 'Groot' (Great) to it, and after that, it was simply known as the Groot Rivier. A Dutch soldier of Scottish extraction, Robert Jacob Gordon, who was commander of the garrison at the Cape in 1777, renamed it the Orange after the Prince of Orange. However, many still referred to it as the Groot Rivier. After the 1994 change of government, it was given back its original name, Gariep.

For many centuries, the early people lived along this river and its tributaries because game was able to graze in the *vleie* and the berry trees and bulbous plants grew in profusion. There, the Korana settled among the Nama herders and groups of San hunter-gatherers. By then, the Korana had become well-armed and some sources cite that they lived very much in the style of the 'Wild West'. They knew how to ride horses, understood the value of keeping their mounts in prime condition, and frequently raided the farms south of the great river and the Baster communities.

They also settled in what is today the Free State, the district that became known as Koranaland (Gordonia). Many small conflicts over hunting and plundering took place between these groups and the Bantu-speaking peoples and White trekkers in the area. It is important to note however, that livestock raids were carried out by a minority group of Korana.

An important leader at the time was Karel Ruyter or Ruiters, an escaped slave, who became chief of the Hoengei group of Gona in the Zuurveld in the mid-eighteenth century.

Other leaders were Piet Rooi, Jan Kupido, Klaas Lukas and Pofadder. Klaas Lukas, who had his headquarters at Olyvenhoutsdrift (Upington), was the most powerful chief.

The small conflicts over cattle and land raids came to a head in 1868, when the colonial government created a special magisterial district. The Northern Border Protection Act was passed to permit action against the Korana. A special border unit was stationed at Kenhardt, but the handful of police and burghers were too few to protect a 330 km stretch of land. This eventually led to the Korana wars of 1869 and 1878.

In 1869, the Frontier Armed and Mounted Police and a small detachment of the Royal Artillery arrived in the area—led by Sir Walter Currie. Together with 400 mounted Boers and Basters, 100 Xhosa and 200 regulars, Currie was soon able to scatter the Korana—but the eluded capture. Klaas Lukas eventually captured the Korana 'raid' leaders and handed them over to the colonial authorities, who banished them to Robben Island. Later, a prolonged drought forced White settlers and Coloured farmers, as well as the Korana, to move closer to the Gariep River. Such a conglomeration of herds close made it easy for Korana 'raider' groups to prey on the herds, and their activities aroused the ire of the district.

Klaas Lukas, who was initially neutral, gathered together 1,000-armed men to defend their livestock. His supporters included the majority of the Korana, the Nama Afrikanders led by Jacobus Afrikander, and a number of Griqua rebels under Gamka Pienaar. The Korana 'raider' groups were defeated and came under the control of the Cape Government. Those Korana who rejected a future under colonial rule trekked further into the Kalahari. The Cape Government settled the Basters near Upington to form a buffer between the

Boers and the Korana. Today, the Korana have almost completely disappeared as a separate group through assimilation with the population in the area.

'Bastaards' or 'Baster' was a derogatory referred to offspring of liaisons between Europeans, slaves and Khoikhoi. The term was also used to refer to subordinate Blacks who could speak Dutch, ride and shoot.

Further Reading

South Africa West Coast History: The Forgotten People from *www.sawestcoast.com*; The Khoisan from *www.khoisan.org*, especially the section on 'raiding'. Chronology. South African History Online.

East, Edward Hyde—Reports of cases argued and determined in the Court of the King's Bencht (1811) Vol XIII.

Elphick, Richard—Khoikhoi and the founding of White South Africa (1985) Ravan Press, Johannesburg, S Africa.

Engelbrecht, JA—the Korana—an account of their customs and their history (1936) Maskew Miller Ltd, Cape Town.

Hunters and herders of southern Africa: a comparative ethnography of the Khoisan peoples by Alan Barnard (Online 'Google Book')

Kennedy, RF—Catalogue of prints in the Africana Museum in the Johannesburg Public Library up to 1870 (1985) Johannesburg Africana Museum 2 Vols.

Knight, Charles, Aborigines in British Colonies, South Africa (1838, London).

Marais, JS, 1968 The Cape Coloured People: 1652–1937 Witwatersrand University Press, Johannesburg.

Miscast: negotiating the presence of the Bushmen by South African National Gallery. Topics as diverse as trophy heads and museums, the destruction of the Cape San, and appraisals of nineteenth-century photographic practices are examined. Pippa Skotnes, was both curator of the exhibit and editor of this volume (Online 'Google Book')

Moodie, Donald—The Record of a series of official papers relative to the condition and treatment of the native tribes of S Africa (MDCCCLX) Cape Town.

Schapaera, Isaac—The Early Cape Hottentots (translations of the writings of Olfert Dapper 1668, Gelielmus de Grevenbroek 1695 and Willem Ten Rhyne 1686 (1930 Routledge & Kegan, London.

Smith, A, 2001 Where have all the Hottentots Gone? The Archaeology and History of the Khoekhoen in Science in Africa, August 2002.

Theal, GM 1908 History of South Africa Since 1795 Sonnenschein & Co, London.

Rare ǂKhomani San Archive Tells a Story of Fragility.

Endnotes

[1] Hoff, JA, *Die Tradisionele Wereldbeskouing van die Khoekhoen* D Phil Thesis, University of Pretoria, 1991 (in Afrikaans).

[2] Macaulay (Lord), the English essayist, is the son of Zacharay Macaulay, the abolitionist whom Saartjie met; Palmer's *Index to the Times Newspaper, 1811.*

[3] Most of Saartjie's human rights were eroded as can be seen when one reads The Universal Declaration of Human Rights, which was adopted by the countries in the United Nations in 1948—long after Saartjie's death, but rights which she was born with: **No 3** The right to live in freedom and safety; **No 4** Not to be enslaved or to enslave; **No 5** Nobody has any right to hurt us or to torture us; **No 6** We all have the same right to use the law; **No 12** Nobody should harm our good name; **No 13** We have the right to go where we want to in our own country and to travel abroad as we wish; **No 22** We all have the right to a home, enough money to live on, to enjoy the arts and make use of our skills; and **No 30** NOBODY CAN TAKE AWAY THESE RIGHTS AND FREEDOMS FROM US.

Name-calling is a known way to cause injury and insult. Saartjie's birth name was never used and has been blocked out of history completely. During her lifetime, she was called Sartje, Saartjie Baartmann, Saartjie Baartman, Sara, Sarah, Sartjee, Saartgee, Sarah Bartmann. The right to her name: a basic human right which Saartjie lost almost at birth!

[4] Human Trafficking is recognised by Interpol as the third largest international crime—after arms and drugs trading. See also BBC News: Published: 2007/03/19 06:13:52 GMT.

[5] Abrahams, Y. *The Great Long National Insult: 'Science', Sexuality and the Khoisan in the early Eighteenth and Nineteenth Century.* Agenda. 32: 34–48. 1997

[6] Khoikhoen or Khoikhoe are other names given to the KhoiKhoi people. They are the aboriginal people of South Africa, also related to the Khoisan ethnic group, the native people of South West Africa (called San or Bushmen) who lived in Southern Africa since the 5th century. Most of the KhoiKhoi have largely disappeared as a group, except for the largest group, the Namas. The KhoiKhoi were pastoralists and agriculturalists on their own land, and stayed in one place, unlike the Khoisan, who were hunters, and moved from place to place (nomads). The two groups are collectively known as the Khoi.

[7] Record of the Examination of Saartjie Baartman filed of record in the King's Bench, London Law Courts—Public Record Office, London, Reference KB1/36 (Xc6367).

[8] Saartjie's skeleton, 'naked and unadorned' stood on public display until 1982 in the Musée de l'Homme, Paris.

[9] *Tata*: Daddy.

[10] Hendrick Cezars, Saartjie's chief schadenfreude, was a freed slave, whom Saartjie had met in South Africa.

[11] Solkar is a character of the author's imagination, a chief's son.

[12] Where the ship, which brought Saartjie to Britain from South Africa, landed, is not known. The author has placed her arrival in the port of Portsmouth. The ship left Cape Town on 20th March 1810 (Kirby, above, 1953).

[13] Cameleopard: a giraffe (Giraffa camelopardalis), an African even-toed mammal, the tallest of all land-living animal species. (*encyclopaedia./thefreedictionary.com*).

[14] *Kaross* is a cloak without sleeves made of sheepskin, or the hide of other animals, with the hair left on. It used to be worn by the Khoikhoi and Bushmen/San peoples of South Africa. These karosses became replaced by a blanket. Their chiefs wore karosses of the skin of the wild cat, leopard or caracal (African lynx)

[15] According to the *Dictionary of National Biography* William Bullock was a traveller, naturalist and antiquarian of some repute. In 1812 he moved his jeweller's business to London and placed his works of art and objects of natural history, which he acquired from Captain Cook, on display in the Egyptian Hall, Piccadilly, which he erected. See Kirby (1949 p56) below. Bullock met Alexander Dunlop for the first time in August 1810.

[16] Hottentot (in English) or *Hotnot* (Dutch), is the derogatory label placed on the indigenous people of South Africa. It used to be the term applied to the Nama people, but Nama is now

the preferred term for the people and their language (Oxford English Dictionary)

[17] *Kraal* is a circular enclosure for cattle or other livestock, located within an African village, surrounded by a mud wall, or other fencing, roughly circular in form.

[18] *Kaptein* is Afrikaans for the Dutch word *Kapteyn*, and English Captain. Saartjie used the term loosely, equivalent to the Chief of her KhoiKhoi tribe.

[19] The young boy actually existed and took Saartjie around in London, according to court records. Obi is his assumed name.

[20] This scene is a construction from the oil painting *The Rabbit Seller* by William Shayer (British, 1787–1879) as documented by David Dabydeen in his essay *Black People in Hogarth's criticism of English Culture* (1992).

[21] Song from *the Universal Songster* (1800) p205.

[22] See Abrahams, Y, above.

[23] *Ramki* is the famous tin guitar called also called a 'blik kitaar' from Southern Africa. During Saartjie's time the body was made from a calabash (see Calabash Footnote 94 below). It is now usually made using an empty oil-can for the body, and is found in South Africa, Botswana and Namibia.

[24] Mr McCartney, Secretary of the African Association, said in Court later that year that he found Saartjie enclosed in a cage on a platform raised about three feet above the floor, and that 'on being ordered by her keeper, she came out, and that her appearance was highly offensive to delicacy,…like a wild beast, ordered to move backwards and forwards and come out and go into her cage, more like a bear in a chain than a human being.' See Altick, RD, above

[25] *John* Philip *Kemble* (1st February 1757–26th February 1823) was an English, Shakesperean, actor. His visit to the exhibition and his comments are true. What transpired between Saartjie and John Kemble is accurately portrayed, as recorded by Mrs Matthews, the wife of Charles Matthews, Comedian, in *Memoirs of Charles Matthews, Comedian,* Vol. 4 (1839, Richard Bently, London, p137).

[26] "The female was clothed in a dress resembling her complexion which is very dark and her dress was so tight that her shapes above and the enormous size of her posterior parts are as visible as if the said female were naked and the dress is evidently intended to give the appearance of her being undressed," said Zachary Macaulay in his Affidavit to the Court. See Affidavit of Zacharay Macaulay, Thomas Gisborne Babington and Peter van Wageninge, Serjeant's Inn, Chancery Lane, London, 17th October 1810, KB/36, Public Records Office, Kew, London "…with no other clothing than a tight dress, the colour of her skin," said 'A Constant Reader' in *The Examiner* of 14th October 1810 p653. Bernth Lindfors (see above) records that she complained to Hendrick Caesar of being too cold (p142).

[27] See Stephen Jay Gold p297 *Flamingo's Smile—Reflections in Natural History,* WW Norton & Co, New York, London (1987).

[28] 'In those days, when bustles were not, she was a curiosity, for English ladies then wore no shape but what nature gave and insisted upon; and the Grecian drapery was simply thrown upon the natural form, without whalebone or buckram to distort or disguise it.' Comment by Mrs Mathews in *Memoirs*

of Charles Mathews, Comedian by Mrs Mathews (1839 Vol iv p.136).

[29] 'This poor female is made to walk, to dance, to shew herself, not for her own advantage, but for the profit of her master who, when she appeared tired, holds up a stick to her, like the wild beast keepers, to intimate her into obedience,' said An Englishman in *The Morning Chronical*, He 'produced a long piece of bamboo, and shook it at her: she saw it, knew its power, and delayed no longer.' Bernth Lindfors (above). Yet, when the Attorney General spoke for her in Court, on 27th November 1810, he said 'She is not desirous of changing her present situation—no personal violence or threats have been used by any individual against her.' See Report of the Examination of the Hottentot Venus—London Law Courts—Public Record Office, London, Ref KB1/36 (XC6367).

[30] Zachary Macaulay, the abolitionist, confirmed this in his Affidavit in Court (above). He said that the 'Exhibitor sometimes would call the said female to him, and when she came would desire her to turn round and would invite the spectators to feel her posterior parts and at other times if she was at a distance from him would desire her to turn round in order that everybody might see her extraordinary shape...'

Mr Matthews, Comedian, said, 'Some of the spectators 'accepted this invitation [to touch Saartjie] by touching her rump and searching for evidence of padding or some other artifice beneath her skimpy, skin coloured dress. A woman who saw the show reported that 'one pinched her, another walked round her; one gentleman *poked* her with his cane; and one *lady* employed her parasol to ascertain that all was, as she called it, *"natural"…On these occasions it required all the authority of the keeper to subdue her.'* (Memoirs of Charles Matthews, above.)

[31] *Baba* – especially among Zulu-speakers: 'father'; used when speaking to or of an older black male who is not necessarily related to the speaker. (Dictionary of South African English.) Saartjie referred to her father as T*ata* – the more familiar 'daddy'.

[32] 'A Constant Reader' in *The Examiner of 14th October 1810 p653.*

[33] Zacharay Macaulay (1768–1838) was a philanthropist. To experience for himself the horrors of 'middle passage', he took passage to the West Indies in a slave ship at some personal risk. After the abolition of the slave trade in 1807 he became secretary of the African Institute without accepting a salary. He was a colleague of Wilberforce, the abolitionist. See *Directory of National Bibliographies* British Library Shelf 2093.c. The conversation in this chapter is transposed from indirect into direct speech as taken from the Affidavit which he made in the subsequent court proceedings above.

[34] The Court records state that 'she had been clandestinely inveigled from the Cape of Good Hope, without the knowledge of the British governor (who extends his peculiar protection in nature of a guardian over the Hottentot nation under his government, by reason of their general imbecile state.' See East, Edward Hyde Vol XIII (1911) pp 195 (quoted verbatim).

[35] This letter was written to Earl of Liverpool. See Theal, McCall George, *Records of the Cape Colony* (1898–) V7 P503.

[36] The Earl of Caledon was Governor of the Cape 1807–1811. He discouraged slavery by selling government slaves and was a popular governor. Caledon, a town in the Western Cape Province, is named after him. *Encyclopaedia of Southern Africa,* Rosenthal 6th Ed, 1973.

[37] It is recorded that Saartjie colluded 'in her own victimisation'. (Bernth Lindfors above). I, Monica, dispute this strongly.

[38] When asked if she wished to see her 4 [sic] sisters and brother, she gave no answer, remained 'inflexibly silent', said Mr Gasalee the Attorney General to the Court at the Final Hearing as reported in *The Morning Post* of Thursday, 29th November 1810.

[39] See Affidavit of William Bullock in the Case of the Hottentot Venus, filed of record in the King's bench, London Law Courts—Public Record Office, London, Ref KB1/36 (XC6367).

[40] Saartjie had no option but to tell the court that the agreement was for six years—see Report of the Examination above.

[41] Autshumao, also known as Herry the strandloper (beach walker), he was chief and interpreter of the Gorinhaikonas. In 1630, he was taken to Bantam by the English and returned to the Cape a year later. He had learned to speak Dutch and English, which made him very useful to his people, and the European settlers who were engaged in a trading relationship.

As result of his position as chief and interpreter of the Gorinhaikonas, he became a rich man.

[42] Krotoa (known as Eva to the Dutch and English settlers) was the niece of Herry. She worked as a servant to the Commander's wife, Maria van Riebeek (nee de la Quellerie) She mastered Dutch and Portuguese and responded eagerly to Christian instruction given her by Maria.

[43] Meneer: Mister.

[44] Now Duke of York Street, a fashionable, good quarter, so named in honour of James, Duke of York, who succeeded to the throne as James II in 1685: *Survey of London* Vol 29 (1960) Part 1.

[45] Veld: field.

[46] See Affidavit by Peter Van Waginenge (of Water Lane, Thames Street, London) and Thomas Gisborne Babington (of the same address as Zacharay Macaulay) dated 17th October 1810 in the Court Records.

[47] Although the court specifically ordered that the interview be held 'in the absence of Alexander Dunlop and Hendrick Cesar', (East, Edward Hyde Vol XIII (1811) p196), The Courier of Thursday, 29th November 1810 recorded that the Court found that 'Mr Dunlop had been kind enough to attend the Master along with two gentlemen who understood the Dutch language.'

[48] The agreement is dated 29th October 1810 between Alexander Dunlop of St James, Middlesex, and Saartjie (Sarah) Baartman, who entered into his employment as a domestic servant. The agreement says that it would begin to run from March of that year for five years. Saartjie is

purported to have agreed, in addition to performing such domestic duties as her master might reasonably demand of her, to allow herself to be viewed by the public of England and Ireland, 'just as she was'. Dunlop agreed to defray all the expenses of the voyage, to give Saartjie, in case of illness, all the care and all such medicines as she might require, and to pay her annual wage of twelve guineas. He also undertook to defray the cost of repatriating her should she desire to return to her country. (Kirby, above, 1953, page 125). Needless to say Saartjie never received any money.

"But it should be known," said Mr Gazely, the Attorney General in Court, "that the Hottentots were supposed so incapable of managing their own concerns, that no contract among them was valid unless it was made before a magistrate and made as usual; but when Lord Caledon discovered for what purpose, he was much displeased, and would have stopped the parties if they had been then in his power," taken from the *Bells Weekly Messenger,* Sunday 2nd December 1810 p 383.

[49] "She understands very little of the Agreement made with her by Mr Dunlop on the twenty ninth October 1810 and which Agreement she produced to us,…and these Deponents were informed by the said female that she could neither read or write," said the Attorney General to the Court on 27th November 1810, reading from the Affidavits of the men who interviewed her, Van Wagininge and Babbington—see above Kirby (1953, above) refutes the agreement, saying that it could not have been drawn up at the Cape, because she was

already in London 'in the course of the autumn of this year' (1810). He said Dunlop had 'shanghaied' her from Cape Town in March of that year, got a lawyer in London, and had the contract prepared without delay, making it retrospective from the date of sailing. Dunlop got off free because of this agreement, which saved him from further responsibility for Saartjie's welfare.

[50] Bernth Lindfors (above p 133).

[51] Paddy is the name I have given to the man she had a child with In *Johnson's Sunday Monitor, British Gazette and London Recorder* of Sunday 2nd December 1810 it says that she had 'an Irish drummer's child' and Walvin, James, et al, 1926 *Black Personalities* British Library Shelf X.809/56557 or X529.70940). Bernth Lindfors (above) also says that she had a child by a drummer at the Cape, 'with whom she lived for about two years, yet being always in the employ Hendrick Caesar' and that the child died.

[52] The first hearing in Court was on a Saturday, 24th November 1810, when the Magistrates ordered that an examination be done of Saartjie, in her own language. The Attorney General pleaded on Saartjie's behalf. No verbatim transcripts of court proceedings were kept in those days, so what happened has been deduced from newspapers at the time. The application to Court was for *habeus corpus*—that is, that the body of a person (in this case 'the Hottentot woman') be brought to court if the keeper does not show why this should not be done, and if he can't show why this should not be done, at the discretion of the Court, they will convey her safely back to her own country. The interview showed why the case failed.

Saartjie was coerced into telling lies and when the court resumed for the second hearing, on 28th November 1810, the case failed because it was reported that Saartjie herself had said that she had no desire to go back to her own country, that she was happy in her situation and that she was waiting for the money promised to her. The case against Cezar and Dunlop was dismissed. I do not believe this is what Saartjie wanted.

[53] Saartjie was baptised under the name Sarah Bartmann in the Parish Church of Christ in Manchester on 7th December 1811 by rev Joshua Brookes. The original baptism certificate is in the Archives of the Musée de l'Homme, Paris. See Kirby above. It has been suggested (Abrahams & Clayton above) that Saartjie consented to baptism. I believe that she had no control over this. I believe that obtaining a baptism certificate for her was a ploy concocted by Hendrick Cezar, because the exhibition was no longer making money, and he wanted to get her to France to sell her there, so he needed papers to get her out of the country.

[54] Saartjie was abandoned by 'An Englishman (Jack Higginbottom who displayed her in Bath, England—see Kirby, *Africana Notes and News*, June 1949 p55 Vol V1, No 3)…and she became the property of a showman in Paris,' says Lloyd, ACG in a letter in *Africana Notes and News*, June 1947 Vol 5 No 3.

[55] In Paris she was exhibited by an animal trainer. See Gould, Stephen Jay *(above)*. His name was Réaux according to Kirby, Percy R in *South African Journal of Science* 1954 July, Vol 50 No 12 P319; and in *Africana Notes & News* 1953,

September Vol X No 4. She was exhibited in a shed in rue Neuve des Petit Champs, Paris for 15 or 16 months (Kirby, above, 1953). See also *Journal des Dames et des Modes* 12th February 1815.

[56] *Sinus pudoris* is the term given to outer vaginal walls that are bigger than normal. It was believed that the Khoikhoi women had these, and scientists tried to prove this by examining and recording the size of the genitalia of women like Saartjie, and this is why they cut out her genitals after her death and preserved them. (Kirby 7/1954 above) They were (and might still be) preserved in the archives of the Musee de l'Homme in Paris. The *sinus pudoris* must not be confused with the little apron which Saartjie always modestly wore as a covering and which the women wore, tied around their waist and hanging down in front. *The sinus pudoris* is misnamed *Hottentot Apron,* but this is completely different from Saartjie's little apron, which she wore at all times, and refused to remove so as to allow examination of her genitalia before her death—see Stephen Jay Gould in *Flamingo's Smile, reflections in Natural History,* 1987, WW Norton & Co, New York, London, pp291–305. The Khoikhoi did not practise intentional labia stretching, usually done by an aunt on girls beginning at the age of four or five, a practice of female genital mutilation.

[57] George Cuvier was a French anatomist, a professor of zoology and physiology who did the autopsy and, amongst other things, made wax moulds of Saartjie's anus, cut out her genitals, and preserved them. See Kirby 1954.7 (above).

[58] See Stephen Jay Gould (above).

[59] Saartjie was born near the banks of the Gamtoos River, in the Eastern Cape, about 30 miles west of Port Elizabeth. Encyclopaedia of S Africa.

[60] !Habab is the Initiation Ceremony.

[61] In 2019, the Eastern Cape Geographical Names Committee recommended that Port Elizabeth be renamed Gqeberha, after the Xhosa and Southern Khoe name for the Baakens River that flows through the city. The city's controversial name change was officially gazetted on 23rd February 2021.

[62] Koppie: Small hill.

[63] Saartjie's father, who was 'in the habit of going with Cattle from the interior of the Cape', was killed in one of those journeys by the 'Bosmen'. See Lindfors above. The details of death and burial were taken from Schapera (see Endnote) 1930 pp360–365.

[64] Bosjeman, also known as Bushman.

[65] Kirie: Stick, walking stick.

[66] *Bosjemans* is a derivative of the Dutch word Boschjesmans or Bushmen in English. "The name 'bushman', or in Dutch, Boschjesmans, was first used as early as 1652 by Dutch settlers to describe the hunter-gatherers they met when they first arrived at the Cape"

[67] The corpse was 'doubled up like an embryo' and wrapped in skins sewn together, Schapera, 1933 (see Endnote).

[68] Straat: Street, which follows its name, e.g. Riebeekstraat.

[69] Duiker is a small African antelope with long hair between its horns. The Dutch word *duiker* means diver, because it has a habit of plunging through bushes when pursued (Oxford English Dictionary).

[70] According to a report by John Barrow, Secretary to Earl McCartney, Governor of the Cape from 1797—in *An Account of Travels into the Interior of Southern Africa* (London, 1801), the status of 'The Hottentots' changed after this. On 1st November 1809 all vestiges of chieftainship were removed and their movements were sharply curtailed. They had to have fixed places of abode, to carry certificates, which had to be produced on demand, and they could not leave their district unless certificates were endorsed by a landdrost (magistrate).

[71] Tokolosh (Tokoloshe, Tokoloshi) is a mythological dwarf zombie. It originally lived in water, and is said to be seen only by children, as a brown or green, hairy dwarf which speaks with a lisp.

[72] Vygie: Wild fig, from the Dutch *vijg*. A succulent groundcover.

[73] Buchu is a small flowering shrub native to South Africa, (Agathosma betulina). The leaves, which are rich in essential oils, have traditionally been used as an herbal remedy and to flavour tea and brandy.

[74] Zoutrivier: Now called Salt River, a suburb of Cape Town, South Africa.

[75] It has been suggested that Saartjie got married and had two children: Fryer, Peter in *Staying Power—The History of Black People in Britain* (1984 Pluto Press) said she had two children from a black man; and Lloyd, ACG in a letter (above) suggested she 'had been married to a negro by whom she had had two children'. I have found no proof of this, especially not in the registry records in the UK, although I have searched quite extensively.

[76] It is not sure what in the end caused Saartjie's death at the very young age of 27 years. Was it smallpox or was a catarrh, a pleurisy [sic], a dropsy of the breast? (Altick above); was it boils (Edwards & Walvin above); or an inflammatory and eruptive sickness (Kirby above 1949, Lloyd above 1947); was it alcoholism? Neglect?

[77] Kirby (above) 1953 – but according to other reports (e.g. Professor Verneau) she died on either on 31st December 1815 or 1st January 1816.

[78] Cuvier 'moulded her entire body in plaster' and made castings. The genital organs and anus were moulded separately in wax. Then he partially dissected the cadaver, and the brain. Etienne Geoffroy St Hilaire was also present at these proceedings. (Kirby, 7/1954 above). The French scientist Geoffroy St Hilaire (Étienne), naturalist (1772–1844) was the co-publisher, with Cuvier, of *Histoire Naturelle des Mammiféres, Paris 1824–57* in which they describe Saartjie under the title 'Femme de Race Bochismann'. A clinic of urology and cardiology in Paris is named after St Hilaire.

[79] Badou, Gerard, *L'enigma de la Venus Hottentote*, Paris, 2000 p133 for full transcript of this letter.

[80] Lawrence, TE, *Seven Pillars of Wisdom*.

[81] Ouma: Grandmother.

[82] Spectators concentrate entirely upon sexual features of the Hottentot Venus. One military gentleman observes her *steatopygia* from behind and comments, "Oh! Godem quel rosbif," said Jay Gould (above).

83 Van der Post, Laurens, ((1906–1996) T*estament to a Bushman.*

84 Affidavit of Zacharay Macaulay, above.

85 Rosseau, Jacques, *Discourse on the Origin of Inequality,* Indianapolis and Cambridge, 1992.

86 Gordon, Robert J, *The Venal Hottentot Venus and the Great Chain of Being*, in African Studies, 51.2.92.

87 Hodgen, Margaret, *Early Anthropology in the Sixteenth and Seventeenth Century,* Philadelphia, Pennsylvania University Press, 1964.

88 Lindfors Bernth, above.

89 Holmes, Rachel, *The Hottentot Venus—The Life and Death of Saartjie Baartman—born 1789–Buried 2002*, Bloomsbury Publishing Plc (2007), p 51.

90 Her master, "…when she appears tired, holds up a stick to her, like the wild beast keepers, to intimidate her into obedience," said 'An Englishman' in the Morning Chronicle, Friday 12th October 1810 p3; "…she is completely under restraint and control and is deprived of her liberty," said Peter Van Wageninge and Thomas Gisborne Babington in their Affidavits to the Court (above).

91 Altick, RD, above.

92 Altick, RD, above.

93 Abrahams, Yvette, *Images of Sara Bartman: Sexuality, Race, and Gender in Early Nineteenth-Century Britain,* in Ruth Roach Pierson and Nupur Chaudhuri, eds, *Nation, Empire, Colony: Historicising Gender and Race* (Bloomington and Indianapolis, 1998).

[94] The Calabash or Bottle Gourd (not to be confused with the calabaza) is a vine grown for its fruit, which can either be harvested young and used as a vegetable or harvested mature, dried, and used as a bottle, utensil, or pipe. The calabash was one of the first cultivated plants in the world, grown not for food but as a container. (Wikipedia.org). See also Kirby, Percival R, *Musical Instruments of the Natives of South Africa* in South African Journal of Science, (1939)36 p481–6.

[95] Campbell, John (Lord), *The Lives of the Chief Justices of England*, Vol 3 (London, 1857) p51.

[96] Wilson, M, *The Hunters and Herders,* in The Oxford History of S Africa (Ed Wilson & L Thompson), 1969, P60.

[97] McCall, George Theal, *Records of the Cape Colony, Vol 7, p 503 (1898).*

[98] A Hottentot of Distinction [unknown], *The Ranelean Religion,* printed in London in MDCCL (1750).

[99] Mathews, Anne (Mrs) (above).

[100] Record of the Examination of Saartjie Baartman, above.

[101] *The Morning Chronicle* 29th November 1810.

[102] Holmes, Rachel, above.

[103] Altick RD, above, gives a detailed description, together with drawings, of various satirical cartoons of Saartjie in *The Noble Savage Revisited* in The Shows of London (1978 Cambridge, Mass. Harvard UP) pp271/2—especially the famous 'Broad Bottom Ministry' cartoon, comparing Saartjie's physique to the generous contours of Henry Pelham of the coalition government in Britain in the 1740s.

[104] Kirby, Percival R, *More about the Hottentot Venus*, in Africana Notes and News Vol X, No 4, September 1953.

Toole-Scott, R, *Circus and Allied Arts,* Derby, 195801971, III.

[105] See cartoon entitled 'A Pair of Broad Bottoms', a coloured engraving published by Walker & Co, 7 Cornhill, London, 1810. This picture of Saartjie, copied from the original drawing by the English cartoonist Frederick Christian Lewis, which is completely uncharacteristic of the small-boned Khoikhoen, appears in the Africana Museum, Johannesburg, as well as in the South African Encyclopaedia, as 'Hottentot Venus'. Her remains were on display in a museum, the *Musee de l'Homme* in Paris until 1982, when they were put into the archives.

[106] Saartjie's final portraits, drawn in the Jardin de Plantes before her death, were drawn by artists Berre, Huet and De Wailly. In 2002 De Wailly's likeness was chosen by the South African government as her official national image, See Rachel Holmes, above, p144.

[107] Kirby, Percival R, *More about the Hottentot Venus*, in Africana Notes and News Vol X, No 4, September 1953.

[108] Gould, Stephen Jay, *(*above*);* Edwards, Paul and James Walvin, *Black Personalities in the Era of the Slave Trade,* Louisiana State University Press 1993.

[109] Holmes, Rachel, (above), p130.

[110] Lloyd, ACG (above), Edwards, Paul, and James Walvin, above. Altick, RD, above.

[111] Altick, R D, above.

[112] Gould, Stephen Jay, above.

[113] Cook, James, *Three Voyages around the World*, Strand, London 1842. See also *The Journals of Captain Cook 1768–1779,* ed Philip Edwards (London) 1999.

[114] Nicholas Culpeper, A Directory for Midwives (1651).

[115] Gordon, Robert J, above.

[116] Cuvier, F, *Report on Observations Made on the Body of a Woman,* (1817).

[117] Kirby, Percival, above.

[118] St Hillaire G and F Cuvier, *Femme de Race Bochismann,* in Histoire Naturelle des Mammiferes, Paris, 1824.

[119] Wilson (1969), above.

[120] Edwards, Paul *London Early 19th Century* (1981).

[121] Edwards, Paul, *Black Personalities in Georgian Britain in History,* in History Today, September 1981. Lindfors, Bernth, above.

[122] The Courier, 29th November 1810.

[123] The Morning Chronical, 26th & 29th November 1810.

[124] Affidavit of William Bullock (above).

[125] The Morning Chronical, 29th November 1810.

[126] The National Register, 2nd December 1810. Bell's Weekly Messenger, 25th November 1810. The Courier, 29th November 1810.

[127] An Englishman in The Morning Chronicle of 12th October 1810.

[128] 'A small stage was erected in the room and some slight scenes, representing an African hut etc, were placed around it; from this hut the poor unhappy woman came forth, like a dog, at the call of its master,' said 'A Constant Reader' in *The Examiner* of 14th October 1810 (p653).

[129] A Constant Reader in The Examiner of 14th October 1810.
[130] Bell's Weekly Messenger, 25th November 1810.
[131] The Courier, 29th November 1810.
[132] Butterworth & K J Cook, *reports of cases argued and determined in the Court of the King's Bench* 1811, 1950196. An Englishman in The Morning Chronicle of 12th October 1810.
[133] Kirby, Percival R, above. The Courier, 29th November 1810.
[134] Chambers, R, *The Book of Days,* London 1879 Vol 2. The Times, 26th November 1810.
[135] The Courier, 29th November 1810.
[136] I dispute the statements made by Stephen Jay Gould in *Flamingo's Smile—reflections in Natural History* (1987, WW Norton & Co, NY, London p293 where he states that Lord Caledon had granted permission; and with Yvette Abrahams & Clayton above where they say that a 'shipping permit' had been granted, which allowed Saartjie to be taken from the Cape. See Lord Caledon's letter, above. Mr Ball, a member of the Africa Society, said in his Affidavit to the Court that Hendrik 'refused to produce Lord Caledon's permission which he had said he had obtained in writing and refused to answer more questions on the subject' in the Report of the Court Hearing in *The Sun* Monday, November 26, 1810. The Attorney General, Mr Gasalee, confirmed this in Court as well. "It was not a fact that Lord Caledon had given his permission," he said as reported in *The Courier,* Thursday, 29th November 1810. *The Morning Chronical* of the same day confirmed this as well. "Mr Dunlop," they said, "had been

kind enough to attend the master along with two gentlemen who understood the Dutch language…"

[137] Hoff, J A, above.

[138] Fryer, Peter *Staying Power—The History of Black People in Britain* (1984 Pluto Press) and Shyllon, Forarin *the Black presence and experience in Britain: An analytical review) p 203.*

[139] Walvin, James *Passage to Britain* (1984). "Large number," he said, "met communally for social activity; some 200 gathered at a ball in 1792, …They looked to themselves for assistance and organisation, rather than their white friends and sympathisers."

[140] Fryer, Peter, *Staying Power—The History of Black People in Britain,* Pluto Press, 1984. Dabydeen, David, *Black People in Hogarth's criticism of English culture,* in Essays in History of Blacks in Britain, Ed Gundara and Duffield, 1992. Shyllon, Forarin, *The Black presence and experience in Britain: An analytical review,* in Essays on the History of Blacks in Britain, before. Walvin, James, *English Urban Life 1776–1851,* 1984.

[141] Walvin, James, above. Cugoano, O, *Thoughts and Sentiments,* London 1787.

[142] Geoffrey Griegson, *The Goddess of Love: The birth, death and return of Aphrodite (also Venus),* London, Quartet Books, 1978.

[143] Lawrence, T E, *Seven Pillars of Wisdom* (Penguin, 1986).

[144] Ferrus, Diana, South African Poet, *I have Come to Take you Home—A Tribute to Saartjie Baartman,* in M C Ndlovu

et al (eds), *A Selection of 21st Century Black Women's Writing from the Tip of Africa (*Cape Town, 2002).

[145] On 9th August (S African Women's Day) in 2002, Saartjie was put to rest in Hankey, near the Gamtoos River, where she grew up.